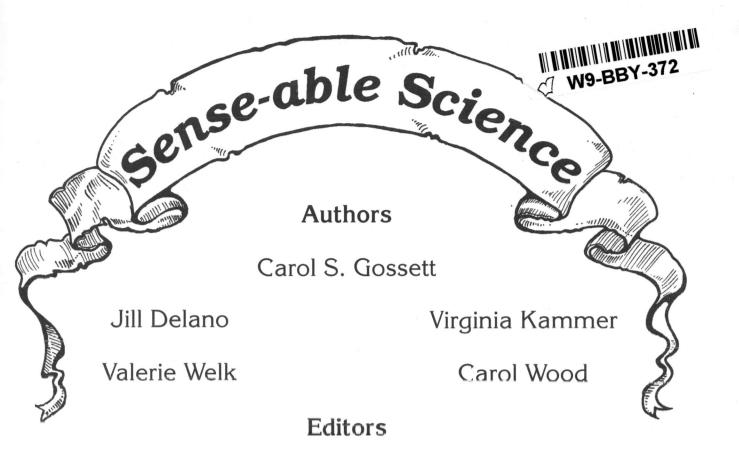

Sense-able Science

Authors

Carol S. Gossett

Jill Delano

Virginia Kammer

Valerie Welk

Carol Wood

Editors

Betty Cordel

Judith Hillen

Illustrator

Margo Pocock

Contributing Artists

Brenda Dahl

Suzy Gazlay

Life Science Consultant

Ben Van Wagner

Desktop Publisher

Leticia Rivera

This book contains materials developed by the AIMS Education Foundation. **AIMS** (**A**ctivities **I**ntegrating **M**athematics and **S**cience) began in 1981 with a grant from the National Science Foundation. The non-profit AIMS Education Foundation publishes hands-on instructional materials (books and the monthly magazine) that integrate curricular disciplines such as mathematics, science, language arts, and social studies. The Foundation sponsors a national program of professional development through which educators may gain both an understanding of the AIMS philosophy and expertise in teaching by integrated, hands-on methods.

ISBN **1-881431-42-8**

Printed in the United States of America

I Hear, and I Forget
I See, and I Remember
I Do, and I Understand

-Chinese Proverb

Table of Contents

Sense-able Science

Our Five Senses

People use their senses to explore and describe their surroundings and themselves.

Most often, senses are used in conjunction with each other.

Sensory perceptions can stimulate emotions and feelings.

Different senses provide different information.

Taste

Humans use their sense of taste to distinguish between sweet, sour, salty and bitter or a combination of the four.

The sense of taste is interrelated with the sense of smell and sight.

Physical and chemical changes in foods caused by heat affect differences in taste through texture and flavor changes.

Smell

Humans find smells to be distinctive, identifiable, and memorable.

The sense of smell can be desensitized.

Touch

The sense of touch enables us to discriminate textures, shapes and sizes.

Sight

Sight enables us to explore patterns and order in our world.

Sight is dependent on the availability of light.

When sight is absent, a human depends on other senses for information.

Hearing

Our sense of hearing enables us to identify the sounds of familiar objects and events.

Sense-able Science Conceptual Overview

The activities in *Sense-able Science* were specifically written to ensure that Kindergarten and First Grade students could explore and discover their five senses. Through the learning processes of observing, sorting and classifying, comparing and contrasting, collecting and recording of data, interpreting data, applying and generalizing, and communicating, the students are allowed to experience their five senses in a developmentally appropriate manner.

Throughout the activities, students become aware that they use their senses to explore their surroundings and themselves; that most often, senses are used in conjunction with each other; that sensory perceptions can stimulate emotions and feelings; and that different senses provide different information.

The organization of the book is by each particular sense. Every section begins with background information for the teacher, an original poem, and song lyrics set to familiar tunes. The activities which follow are filled with multi-disciplinary components.

Science

Life Science is the foundation of this book with specific concepts addressed in each lesson. Some examples are:

- The concept that sight enables us to explore patterns and order in our world is found in *Peeking At Patterns*.
- Students find that sight is dependent on the availability of light in the activity *I See The Light*.
- In activities such as *Touch And Tell* and *Shape Search* students find that when sight is absent, they depend on other senses for information.
- *Walk, Stop, and Listen* takes students on a blindfolded walk to see if they can identify their locations. Through this experience, they will find that their sense of hearing enables them to identify the sounds of familiar objects and events.
- *Texture Rough, Texture Smooth* and *Bags Of Beads* were designed to show students that they can discriminate textures, shapes, and sizes by using their sense of touch.
- In *Taste Bud Mapping* students will taste sweet, sour, and salty flavors to find that there are specific areas on their tongues where each taste can be distinguished.
- Finding that the senses of taste and smell are interrelated is enjoyable as students do taste tests in *The Art Of Tasting*.
- *Make Mine Porridge* allows students to see the change in the texture of cereals through cooking.
- Students find that smells are distinctive, identifiable, and memorable in *Canned Scents* and *Making Sense Of What You Smell*.
- *The Napping Nose* informs students that their sense of smell can be desensitized.

Mathematics

Mathematical concepts are embedded throughout the activities. Students tally and compare results, they use measurement in cooking experiences, geometry and spatial sense are utilized while studying the shapes of beads and sandpaper cutouts. The use of counting, numeration, whole number operations, and identifying equalities and inequalities permeate the entire experience. By using time intervals, Kindergartners and First Graders become acquainted with the use of the clock as a measuring tool. Students collect and record data in various ways: in charts, in graphs, in Venn diagrams with mathematical interpretations that naturally follow.

Social Sciences

The social science component of the book is an important aspect in each activity as the students interact with each other, their families, and their environment. Through *Home Links*, students are encouraged to extend the activities into the home setting thus encouraging further participation.

An awareness of similarities and differences among people is dealt with not only in the activities themselves, but also in the illustrations and the recommended literature found in the *Bibliography*. Other comparisons are made between humans and other animals while studying the sense of sight (*The Eyes Have It*) and hearing (*Designer Ears*).

Students simulate the loss of sight through the use of blindfolds (*Home Free*), the loss of touch through the use of gloves (*Kid Gloves*), and the loss of hearing by covering their ears with their hands (*Direction Detection*). They discover the importance of one sense through the loss of another. They also learn that the senses work together to enhance the effectiveness of their bodies to survive in their world.

Literature

The literature connections have been carefully chosen for their content and "message" to the students in your classrooms. Activities such as *Make Mine Porridge, Egg-stra Special Scramble,* and *Walk, Stop, and Listen* were written for use with specific titles: *Goldilocks and the Three Bears, Green Eggs and Ham,* and *The Listening Walk.* Reference to many other books is made both in conjunction with individual activities and in the *Bibliography*.

Art and written and oral communication are used for recording what students have learned. Special journals have been designed for many of the activities in which students can record and reflect on their experiences.

Fine Arts

Artistic expression is encouraged through the use of music and poetry. Each section of *Sense-able Science* includes an original poem and song lyrics which help to link science content to real-world experiences.

Written and Oral Language

Communication, through the use of oral and written language and art, is used in specially designed journals. When students are provided with the opportunity to record and reflect upon an experience, the increased exposure enables them to strengthen their understanding of the concepts being learned. This opportunity for individual reflection also presents the teacher with an occasion for assessment as to the understandings and misconceptions held by that student.

Assessment

Assessment has been integrated into the instructional procedures of the activities. The use of journals, further investigations, oral interpretations, purposefully designed discussion questions, and performance-based tasks are some examples of the types of assessment imbedded within the activities. The assessment components are designed to reflect the student's conceptual understandings, not the ability to recall facts or memorize vocabulary. Assessment in *Sense-able Science* emphasizes depth of knowledge, not quantity of knowledge.

Sense-able Science Lines Up

	Math/Science Processes											Math												Science				
	Observing	Contrasting and comparing	Gathering and recording data	Sorting and classifying	Communicating	Applying	Generalizing	Inferring	Interpreting data	Making and testing hypotheses	Predicting	Charting	Estimating	Graphing	Identifying and analyzing patterns	Identifying and using inequalities	Measuring	Ordering	Tallying	Using geometry and spatial sense	Using logical thinking	Using number sense and numeration	Using whole number operations	The sense of sight	The sense of hearing	The sense of smell	The sense of taste	The sense of touch
Home Free	●	●	●						●	●	●	●	●							●		●		●				
I See the Light	●	●	●			●			●															●				
Peeking At Patterns	●	●	●		●				●		●	●	●							●				●				
Rainbow 'Round My Room	●	●	●	●					●			●											●	●				
Color My World	●	●	●	●					●													●		●				
Water Colors	●	●	●	●					●			●												●				
The Eyes Have It	●	●	●	●		●			●															●				
Shape Search	●	●	●	●			●		●	●	●									●		●	●					●
Touch and Tell	●	●	●	●	●				●		●				●				●			●						●
Texture Rough, Texture Smooth	●	●	●	●					●		●							●				●						●
Kid Gloves	●	●	●						●	●	●				●							●		●				●
Bags of Beads	●	●	●	●									●						●									●
You Tickle My Fancy	●	●	●		●		●		●		●				●							●						●
Seeing Is Not Always Believing	●	●		●		●	●			●	●	●									●						●	
Eggs-Tra Special Scramble	●	●	●						●		●		●								●						●	
Make Mine Porridge	●	●	●					●	●				●				●				●	●					●	
The Art of Tasting	●	●	●		●	●			●									●				●					●	
Taste Bud Mapping	●	●	●			●			●		●		●														●	
Canned Scents	●	●	●	●					●		●	●	●		●											●		
The Napping Nose	●	●	●						●		●		●				●					●				●		
Making Sense of What You Smell	●	●				●				●	●	●														●		
Making Scents From Scratch	●	●																								●		
Secret Sounds	●	●	●						●	●	●		●												●			
Walk, Stop, and Listen	●	●	●	●					●			●				●									●			
Designer Ears	●	●			●			●	●																●			
Direction Detection	●	●	●			●		●	●									●				●			●			
Paper Picnic	●	●	●	●	●	●			●			●		●				●						●	●	●	●	●

To the teacher...

The activities in this publication provide an integrated approach for the Kindergarten and First Grade curriculum. We have purposefully woven together math, science, and social science concepts with music, poetry, oral and written communication, literature, and artistic expression. Our guiding documents for this multi-disciplinary book were *Science for All Americans* and *Benchmarks for Science Literacy* (American Association for the Advancement of Science), *Curriculum and Evaluation Standards for School Mathematics* (National Council of Teachers of Mathematics), the AIMS *Model of Learning* and *Thinking Skills*.

Even though we acknowledge that our senses tell us about our world, we usually take them for granted because we don't normally think about them. With *Sense-able Science* we hope you will be able to teach students about how their senses provide them with very important information. Through this knowledge, we trust that they will be careful to protect their senses to more thoroughly enjoy their world.

We encourage teachers who use Sense-able Science to be mindful of children with handicaps and enlighten others as to the obstacles these challenged children must overcome as well as the successes they experience.

Sincerely,

The Writing Team

Sense-able Science

An Overview of the Five Senses

Are you ever amazed when you consider how we function day by day? We interact with our environment and control our own bodies. We do this by performing three operations: 1) we perceive our world with our senses, 2) we receive and process the information from our senses through our nervous system, 3) we react to that processed information with our muscles and skeletal system. To simplify, we smell the chicken grilling on the barbecue, our brain tells us that our stomach is not full, and we fill our plate to eat—we sense, we process, and we react!

In the primary grades, students learn a simplified classification scheme of the human's five main senses—touch, taste, smell, seeing, and hearing—which provide them with information about their world. Each of these five senses has a sensory organ associated with it: The organ for touch is the skin, the organ for taste is the tongue, the organ for smell is the nose, the organ for seeing is the eye, and the organ for hearing is the ear. These organs contain receptors which receive information and relay it as electrical signals called nerve impulses to the brain.

Nerves carry the impulses of information from the sensory organs to the brain. The thalamus, a small region in the center of the brain, is the first stop for many impulses. It helps to sort out, interpret, and compare the information from the different sensory organs. The thalamus acts like a post office, which sorts the letters it receives and sends them to the correct addresses.

Information is sent from the thalamus to various sensory centers of the cerebral cortex. The cortex is a very thin layer which covers the top and sides of the brain. Impulses from each sense are localized in discrete regions of the cortex where their information is received and processed. Severe brain damage may cause particular sensory losses, such as blindness or deafness. Since brain cells cannot normally reproduce, once a region of the brain is destroyed, such sensory losses are often permanent. In some cases, however, training can cause other undamaged regions of the cortex to take over some of the lost functions.

Sight

Have you ever watched a bird soar in the sky or the spray created behind a moving truck after a rain? Have you ever looked closely at the petals of a rose? Sights such as these are common enough that often we hardly pay any attention to them; yet the ability to see sights such as these is a marvel in itself. Vision allows us to view the light from stars that are billions of miles away and to thread a needle. Our sense of sight profoundly affects our lives. Eighty percent of the information received by the brain comes in through our eyes. Our sense of sight enables us to know the size and shape of objects, how near they are, and how fast they are going.

Our sense of sight is the most highly developed of the five senses studied in this book. Light enters the eye through an opening called the pupil. It is focused by a lens and projected onto the retina at the back of the eyeball. The retina contains the light-sensitive receptors called rods and cones which convert the light into nerve impulses. The nerve impulses are sent along the optic nerve to the brain.

The vision center of the brain is located at the back of the cerebral cortex. Information from the receptors is sifted, coordinated and interpreted here.

I Can't Imagine

I can't imagine being blind
What things I couldn't do or see
But I think I know someone who'll
Explain it all to me.

I know a man who has a dog
To guide him where he needs to go,
Who sees the steps and holes and curbs
And tells his master so.

Ruff goes along to restaurants,
Rides buses, goes to school.
When it's not safe to cross a street,
He's stubborn like a mule.

My friend can use his fingertips
To read his favorite books;
Small "letter bumps" form words in Braille
They're handy when he cooks.

The Braille knobs on his kitchen stove,
The Braille watch on his wrist,
Help him to do what I can do
Without sight, there's the twist.

Another thing he does that's neat
To know how much he spends,
Is fold his money different ways
To tell the fives from tens.

By counting steps around his house,
He knows how it's arranged;
And he can find things easily
As long as nothing's changed.

There's one thing he finds funny, too,
How some folks speaking to him yell.
They seem to think, that since he's blind,
His hearing's gone as well!

So, when I think about my friend,
I'm grateful I can hear and see.
But now I know if I could not,
I'd learn to do things differently.

Brenda Dahl

My Eyes Can See

Tune: Down by the Bay

I have two eyes
So I can see;
So many things
Look good to me.
I look around
And I can see
The world is full
Of such wonderful things.
My eyes can see!

My eyes are brown
Or blue or gray
Or black or green;
They're made that way.
I look at you,
You look at me,
Our eyes are made
Such a wonderful way
So we can see!

My eyes need light
So I can see
Such colors bright
Are there for me.
Just look around
And you'll agree,
The world is full
Of such beautiful things.
Our eyes can see!

Words by Suzy Gazlay

Home Free

Topic
The sense of sight

Key Question
How does the loss of sight affect whether or not we can put the squirrel in its hole in the tree?

Learning Goal
The students will learn that the sense of sight orients them to their environment and allows them to interact with their surroundings.

Guiding Documents
Project 2061 Benchmark
- *People use their senses to find out about their surroundings and themselves. Different senses give different information. Sometimes a person can get different information about the same thing by moving closer to it or further away from it.*

NCTM Standards 2000*
- *Count with understanding and recognize "how many" in sets of objects*
- *Represent data using concrete objects, pictures, and graphs*
- *Describe parts of the data and the set of data as a whole to determine what the data show*

Math
Using number sense and numeration
Estimation
Geometry and spatial sense
Graphing

Science
Life science
    human senses

Integrated Processes
Observing
Comparing and contrasting
Predicting
Collecting and organizing data
Interpreting data

Materials
For the class:
    one large tree pattern
    one large squirrel pattern
    class graph

For each student:
    blindfolds (see *Management 2*)
    2 small sticky dots
    1 large sticky dot
    student journal
    squirrel graph marker

Background Information
    Sight is the human sense which provides us with the most information about our world. The eyes are an inlet for images. Our brains interpret these images and provide us with information about our spatial relationships in the environment. In this activity, students will be blindfolded and attempt to put a paper squirrel in the hole of a tree. The students will therefore become aware of how their sense of sight plays a major role in their everyday activities.

Management
1. This activity is best demonstrated for the whole class and then done with small groups at a station.
2. Use personal blindfolds so as not to chance the spread of any eye diseases (for a blindfold pattern, see *Appendix: Science Tools*).
3. Prepare one journal per student. Cut and fold the

cover page leaving the pictures on the outside of the fold. Cut and fold the inside page positioning the pictures to be on the inside of the fold. Glue the inside page to the back of the cover page. A book will be formed with a squirrel on the cover page, a tree for predicting as the second page, a tree for recording actual results as the third page, and the back page *What I learned.*

4. Tape the three sections of the tree pattern together and mount entire tree to a large piece of butcher paper. and attach to a wall, bulletin board, door or easel. The tree pattern can be colored and laminated so that it can be used from year to year.

5. Copy squirrel picture onto tag or heavy paper. Laminate it for durability.

6. Copy enough squirrel graphing markers so that each student will have one.

7. The graphing for this activity can be done in either of two ways: by enlarging the student graph or by using the enlarged labels and title provided for an AIMS 3-column graph.

Procedure

1. Invite a small group of students to bring their blindfolds to the station. Give them a journal and direct them to write their names on the front cover in the squirrel's tail.

2. Show them the laminated picture of the squirrel and the tree. Tell them that when they are blindfolded, they will try to put the squirrel in the hole of the tree. Have them turn to page 2 of their journals and place a small sticky dot to predict where they think they will be able to put the squirrel.

3. Blindfold a student, turn him or her around two times. Give the student the squirrel and head him or her in the direction of the tree.

4. Use a sticky dot to mark where the student first places the squirrel.

5. Remove the blindfold and have the student mark his or her initials in the sticky dot.

6. With the second small sticky dot, have the student indicate the actual placement of the squirrel on the third page of the journal.

7. As each student finishes marking the actual placement of the squirrel, have him or her place a squirrel graphing marker in the appropriate column on the graph.

8. After all the students have had a turn, invite the entire class to sit in a large circle to discuss where the dots were placed.

9. Students may copy the data from the large class graph onto their own individual graph, using x's or their own sketches of squirrels to represent the squirrel markers. These can be taken home to share with their families.

Discussion

1. Which of the five senses did we not use? [sight, we were blindfolded]

2. Why was this difficult without sight?

3. What information does our class graph tell us?

4. Without the sense of sight, what things would we miss knowing about our world?

5. Do you know of any children who do not have the sense of sight? What do they do to make up for not being able to see?

6. How can we best know about our world?

7. If we did this again without the blindfold, how many students do you think would be able to put the squirrel in the hole?

8. How does the loss of sight affect whether or not we could put the squirrel in its hole in the tree?

Extensions

1. Let students try using two senses, such as hearing and touch. The sense of hearing can be added by letting a child pretend to be a bird and softly chirp beside the tree. Touch can be added by not marking where the students first put the squirrel, but by letting them feel around for the tree.

2. Use other animals: a bear and a cave, a bee and a hive, a bird and a nest. This can be made seasonally appropriate to integrate into a class theme.

Curriculum Correlation

Literature:
   Hoberman, Mary Ann. *A House Is A House For Me.* Puffin Books. NY. 1993.

Language Arts:

1. Brainstorm ideas of why the squirrel would need to quickly find its home and what senses it uses to find it.

2. Read books about animals that live in trees.

Home Link

1. Play pin the tail on the donkey.

2. With a brother, sister, or parents as guides, have students try to walk around their houses while they are blindfolded.

7

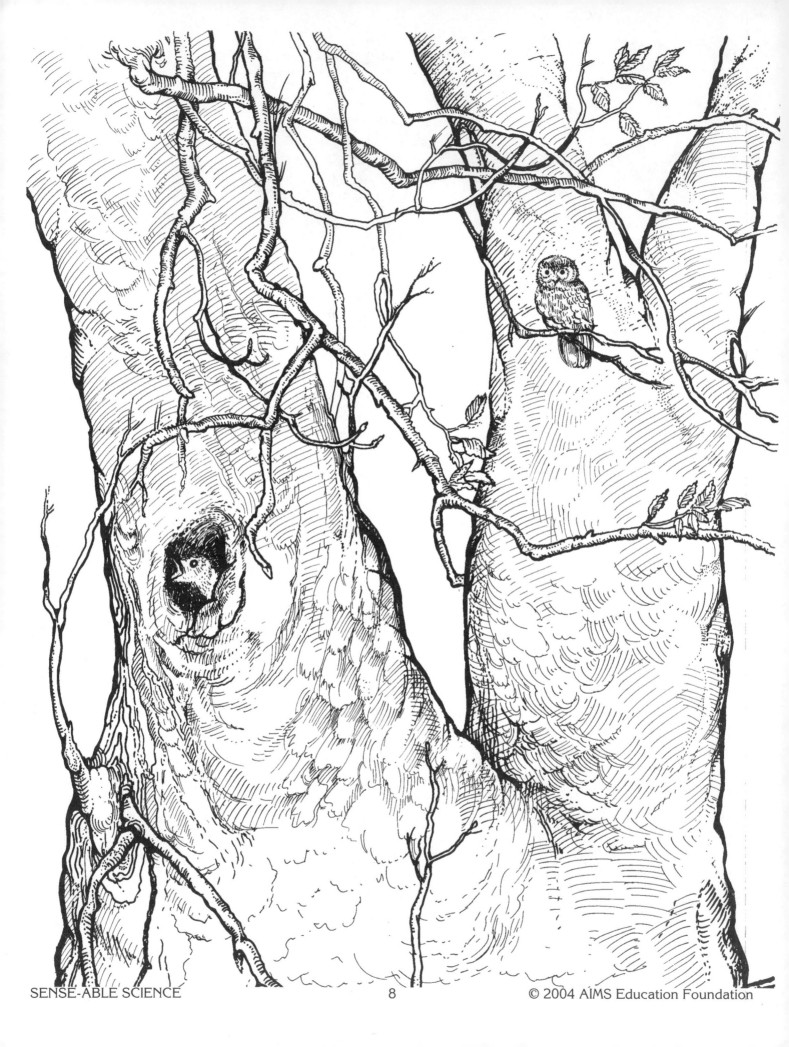

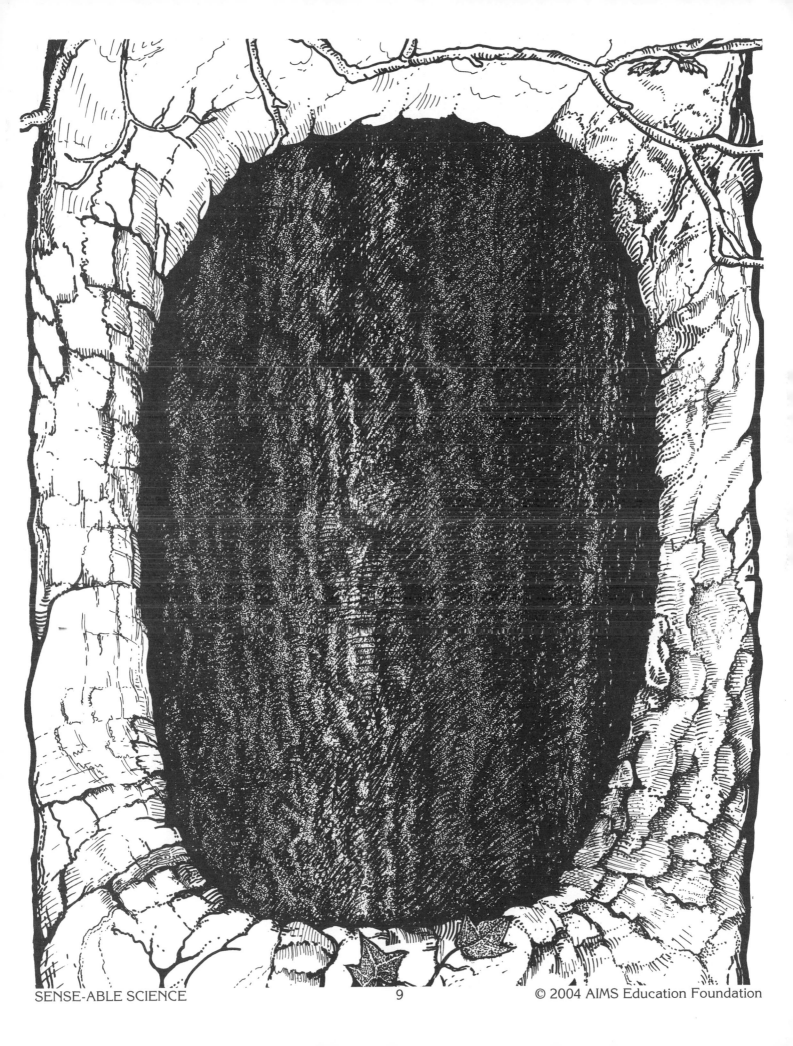

9

10

Home Free

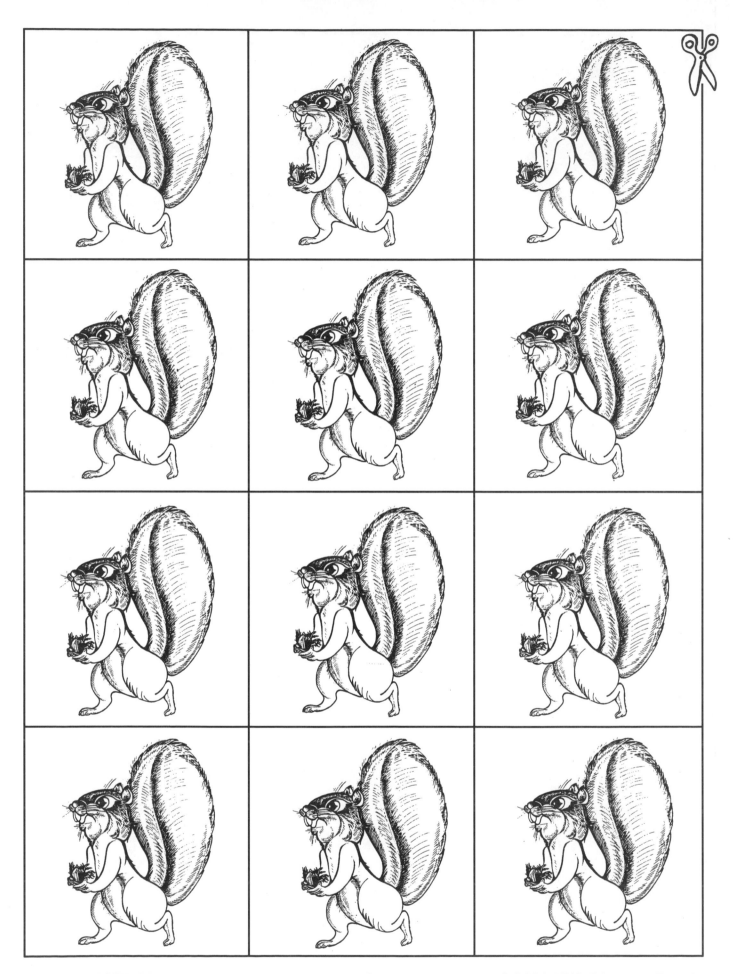

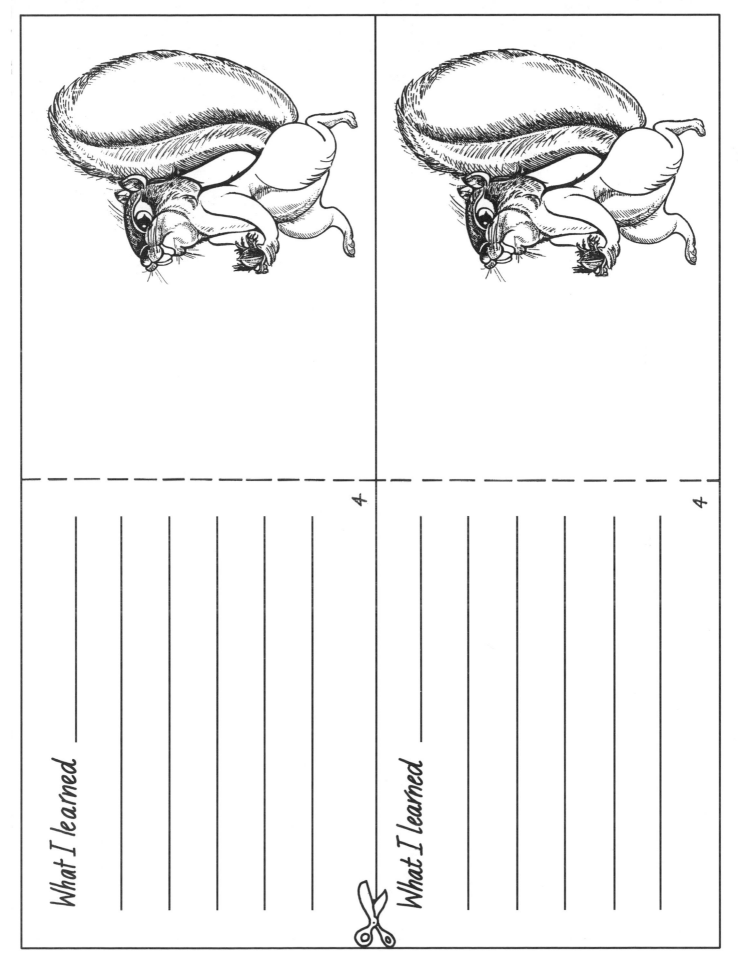

4

4

What I learned _____

What I learned _____

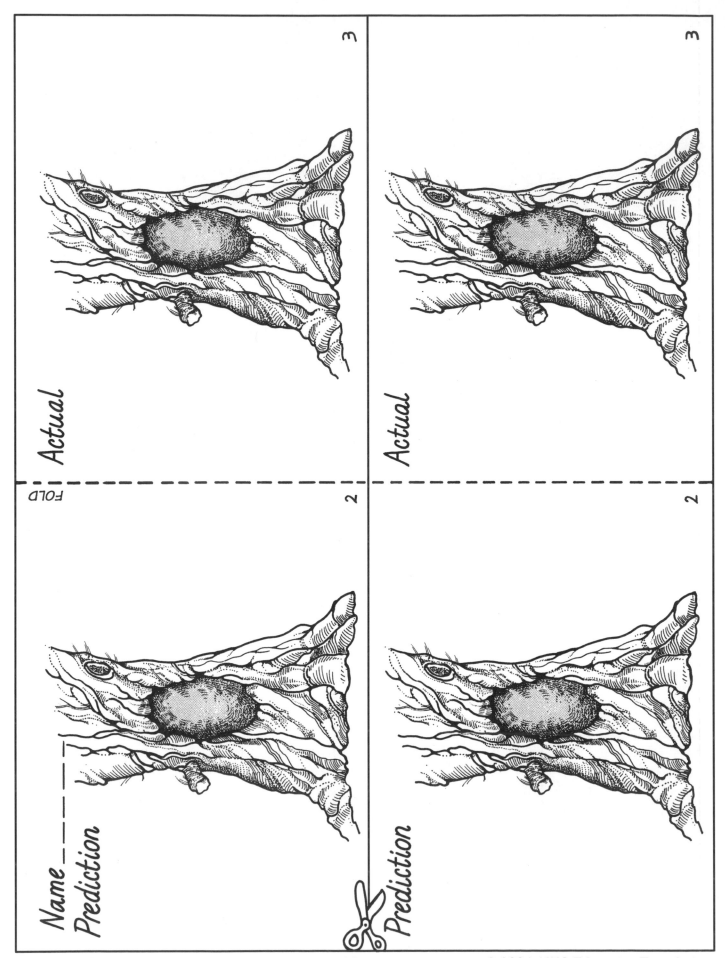

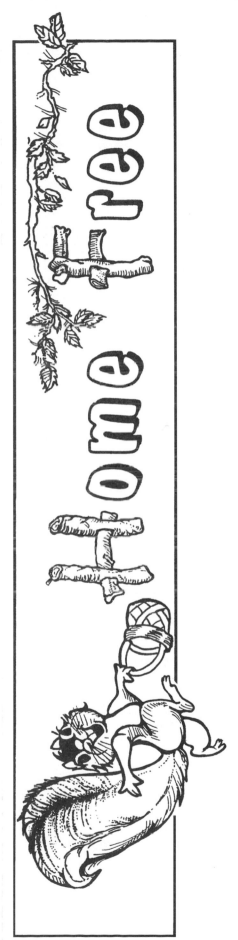

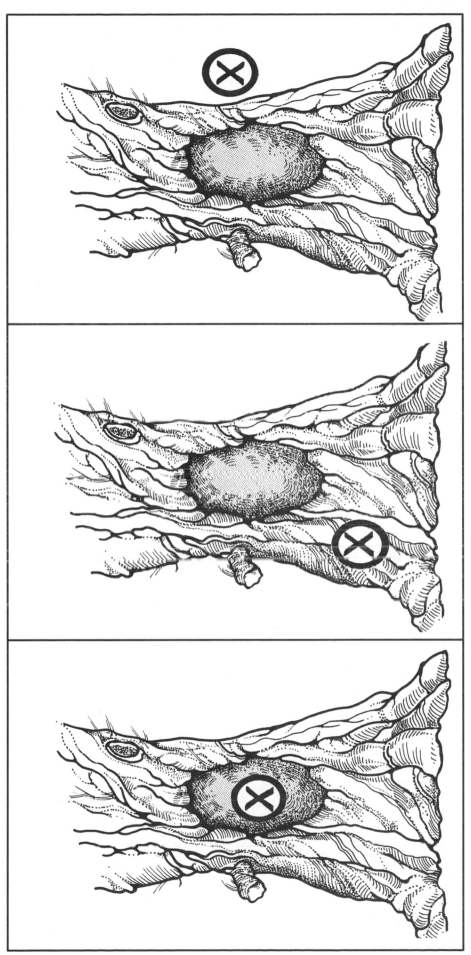

I See the LIGHT

Topic
Sense of sight

Key Question
What do your eyes need in order to see?

Learning Goal
Students will discover that our eyes need light for them to see objects.

Guiding Document
Project 2061 Benchmark
- *People use their senses to find out about their surroundings and themselves. Different senses give different information. Sometimes a person can get different information about the same thing by moving closer to it or further away from it.*

Science
Life science
   human senses

Integrated Processes
Observing
Comparing and contrasting
Recording data
Interpreting data
Applying

Materials
For the class:
   eight boxes
   teacher-made dioramas *(see Management 2)*

For each student:
   recording sheets
   crayons

Background Information
Our eyes contain photoreceptors, specialized sensory cells that detect light and differences in light intensity. These sensory cells are called rods and cones. Rods are much more light-sensitive than cones. Vision in dim light, such as moonlight, is almost entirely due to reception by the rods. There are three different types of cones, each one sensitive to a different color of light; together they provide color vision. With no light, we are unable to see. With dim light, colors are difficult to detect.

Management
Prior to the activity:
1. Boxes which can be completely closed are necessary for this activity.
2. Glue or tape objects into each of eight boxes (see *Figure 1*) to make a diorama.

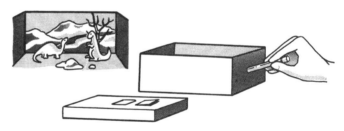

Figure 1

3. Use a pencil to poke a small hole at one end of the box for a "peep" hole.
4. Cut two flaps on the top of the box that can be opened and closed. The size of the flap depends on their placement and the size of the box. Try to place the flaps near the middle of the top of the box.

Procedure
Small group instruction:
1. Ask your students what they use to see.
2. Tell them that you are going to pass some boxes around and they are to peek into each box. (The flaps should be closed.) They are then to draw a picture of what they see on their recording pages in the space marked *First I See.* (This will usually be a black drawing.)

3. After students have peeked into the boxes and made their responses on their pages, demonstrate how to open one of the top flaps on their boxes.

4. Tell your students to pass the boxes around their group and to peek into the box with one flap open and to record their answers in the appropriate *Second I See* space. (Students should be able to see silhouettes.)

5. Once all the students have recorded their observations, tell them to open the second flap on the top of the box and to once again pass the box around. Instruct the students to record their observations in the *Third I See* space. (Students should be able to see definite pictures with color.)

6. Finally, allow the students to draw a design of a "peep box" they would like to make to share with other students.

Discussion

1. Was your first drawing the same as your second?
2. Why do you have different drawings when you looked at the same thing three times?
3. What was different about the box the second time you looked into it?
4. What did your eyes need in order to see the objects in the box?
5. When could you see color: The first, second, or third time you looked into the box?
6. What did your eyes need more of to see the color? [light]

Extensions

1. Have groups exchange boxes and repeat the activity.
2. Allow the students to design and build their own "peep boxes" and record what they can see in them with different amounts of light. Allow them to pass the boxes around to other groups. Have the students record what they see with *no light, a little light,* and *more light.*
3. Find a room at school (bathroom, teacher supply room, a room on stage, etc.) that can be made very dark. Take the students, in pairs, into the room and turn a light on. Ask them to count how many fingers their partner is holding up. Turn out the lights and again ask them to determine the number of fingers their partners are holding up. Again, they will see that light is needed for them to even see their partner next to them.

Curriculum Correlation

Literature:
see *Bibliography: Sense of Sight*

Home Links

1. Send the assignment of designing and building their own "peep boxes" home and make it a family project. Ask the students to bring their creations back to school to share with others.
2. Instruct the students to try to see in their bedrooms at night when all the lights are out. If they can still see, ask them to find out where the light is coming from that is helping them to see (outside street lights, lights in another room, the hall light, a night light, the moon, etc).

I See the LIGHT

First I see

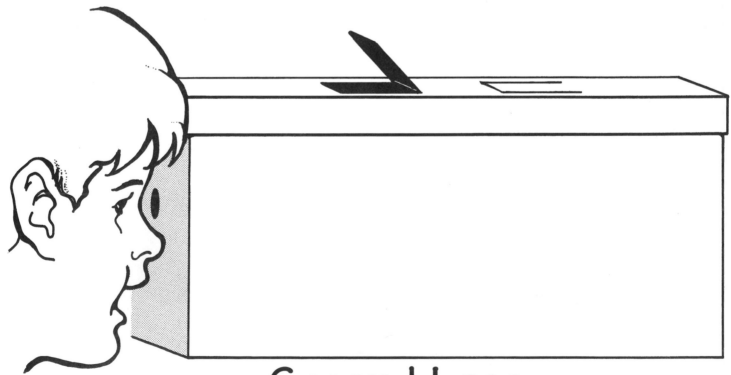

Second I see

I See the LIGHT

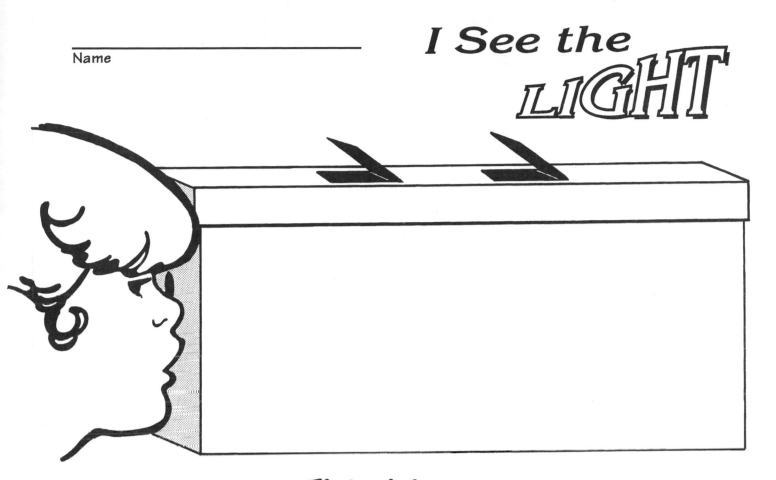

Third I see

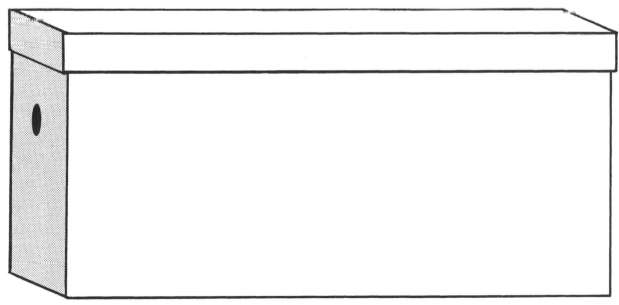

A plan for my own peek box

PEEKING AT PATTERNS

Topic
The sense of sight

Key Questions
1. What sense do we use when we look for patterns?
2. What will we discover on our pattern walk today?

Learning Goal
Students will look for patterns inside and outside the classroom.

Guiding Documents
Project 2061 Benchmark
- *Circles, squares, triangles, and other shapes can be found in things in nature and in things that people build.*

NCTM Standards 2000*
- *Recognize, describe, and extend patterns such as sequences of sounds and shapes or simple numeric patterns and translate from one representation to another*
- *Analyze how both repeating and growing patterns are generated*
- *Sort and classify objects according to their attributes and organize data about the objects*
- *Represent data using concrete objects, pictures, and graphs*
- *Select and use appropriate statistical methods to analyze data*
- *Describe parts of the data and the set of data as a whole to determine what the data show*

Science
Life science
   human senses

Math
Geometry and spatial sense
Math patterns
Graphing

Integrated Processes
Observing
Comparing and contrasting
Predicting
Collecting and organizing data

Interpreting data
Communicating

Materials
Crayons or felt pens
Student clipboard (see *Appendix: Science Tools*)
Large piece of butcher paper
35 pieces of 3" x 11" paper
Student journals (see *Management 2*)

Background Information
Patterns occur everywhere, both in natural and manmade things. To help students understand patterning, they should be exposed to and encouraged to discuss both types. This lesson is to be used after the children understand patterning and is intended to be an extension of patterning into their real world.

Management
1. Prior to doing this activity, prepare a large class graph by either using butcher paper or the enlarged two-column graphs available from AIMS. Divide the graph into two parts labeled *Indoors* and *Outdoors*. This graph will be used for organizing the patterns recorded by the students.
2. Prepare one student journal for each student by cutting the provided journal pages and folding so that the picture of the boy looking at patterns in nature is on the front cover. Fold the blank pages so that they fit inside the first section. Glue, or staple, along the left-hand side to form a book.
3. This activity is divided into four parts. The first three parts use the same student-made pattern pictures. The fourth part, *Student Journals*, is used as an assessment.

Procedure
Part 1
1. Review the concept of patterning with the students.
2. Provide each student with a strip of the 3" x 11" paper, a crayon or felt pen, and the personal clipboard.
3. Take students on a pattern walk by first going around the room and then, weather permitting, outdoors. Encourage students to identify patterns as they see them.

4. Discuss with the students that they are using their senses of sight in doing this activity.

5. Ask the students how they can record their patterns so they can share them with others? Allow time to discuss the problem and lead them into suggesting that they draw the patterns. Invite students to draw patterns with their crayons or felt pens. Encourage them to make their drawings as complete as possible. Be certain to allow students enough time to share the patterns with the rest of the class.

6. When the drawing and individual sharing are finished, have the students sit in a large sharing-circle with their drawings held in their laps. Ask the students how the patterns could be organized so they can be shared with the entire class. Allow students to openly discuss this problem. If necessary, lead them to suggest using a graph.

7. Introduce the prepared graph and discuss the labels of *Indoors* and *Outdoors*. If your students suggest other labels, be prepared to allow them time later to design their own labels. It is important for the students to become graphers, not just graph readers.

8. Have students place their pictures in the appropriate columns of the graph.

Part 2:
1. Using the same patterning pieces, do a second graph. This time graph by number of parts to the patterns: two, three, or four.

Part 3:
1. Using the students' original pattern drawings, ask them for suggestions as to how to organize the patterns in yet another way [patterns with shapes, patterns with colors, patterns with shapes and colors]

Part 4:
1. As an assessment, use the student journals to represent patterns. Depending on the developmental abilities of your students, instruct them to draw samples of patterns representing a two-part, three-part, and four-part pattern Design this part of the activity to meet the needs and abilities of your students.

Discussion
1. Discuss the *Key Questions*: What sense did we use when we looked for patterns? What did we discover on our pattern walk?
2. What was the same in your pattern and your classmates' patterns? What was different?
3. Were *Indoor* or *Outdoor* patterns observed the most? How do you know? Why do you think there were more patterns in one area than another?

4. What other areas could we explore to find patterns? Make a list of places to investigate.

Extensions
1. Make a class book of patterns that were made while on the pattern walk.
2. Photograph patterns around the school and display them for discussion.
3. Contrast and compare patterns seen at various times of the year.
4. Have students arrange themselves into patterns using various attributes: gender, types of shoes, colors of shirts, etc.

Curriculum Correlation
Literature:
1. Read *Dots, Spots, Stripes, and Patterns* by Tana Hoban.
2. Read other books by Tana Hoban.
3. see *Bibliography: Sense of Sight*

Language Arts:
  Chart the patterns from the Hoban books.

Art:
  Make a pattern mural using patterns observed on walks.

Home Link
1. Ask the students to record patterns they observe at home and to bring them back to school to share via a class graph.
2. Ask the students to find a piece of clothing at home which shows a pattern and wear it for a special "Pattern-Me" Day.

INDOORS

OUTDOORS

Cut out and use these labels for graphs.

2 Parts

3 Parts

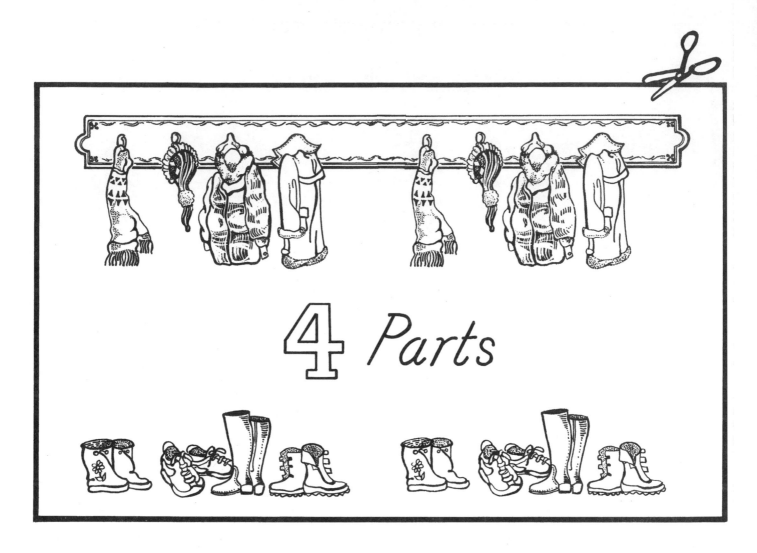

4 Parts

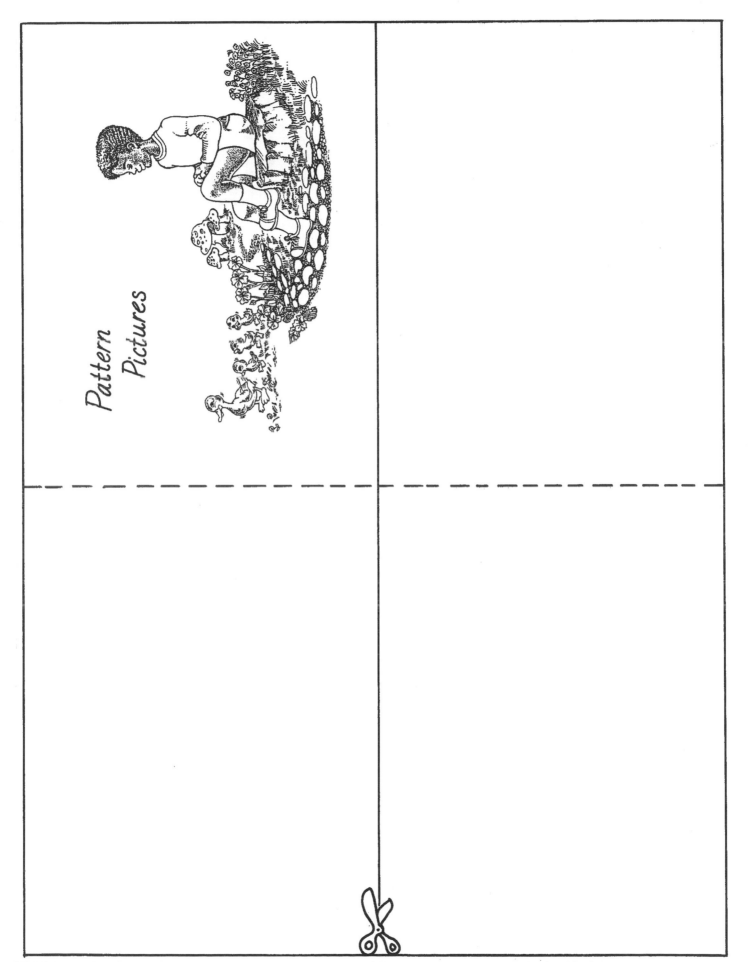

Pattern Pictures

PEEKING AT PATTERNS

I went out for a walk today
And all about me on the way.
Were patterns left for me to find
Of every size and shape and kind.

In looks, four houses, just the same
Sit side by side along our lane.
Each has two windows, next a door,
A walking, steps, two windows more.

And at each fence the flowers grow
Planted neatly in a row,
Pink, white, red, a tree and then,
Pink and white and red again.

My stomach says, "It's time for lunch!"
And so I gather in a bunch
Three flowers each, pink white and red
For Mom from my own flower bed.

Inside, the flowers in a vase,
With dishes matched at every place,
I see again, to my surprise,
New patterns right before my eyes.

And affter lunch is cleared way
I make a picture of my day,
With houses just alike you see.
The only difference is me!

Brenda Dahl

26

Rainbow 'Round My Room

Topic
Sense of sight

Key Question
How many rainbow colors can we find in our room?

Learning Goal
Students will become aware that they use their sense of sight to detect colors.

Guiding Documents
Project 2061 Benchmark
- *People use their senses to find out about their surroundings and themselves. Different senses give different information. Sometimes a person can get different information about the same thing by moving closer to it or further away from it*

NCTM Standards 2000*
- *Sort and classify objects according to their attributes and organize data about the objects*
- *Represent data using concrete objects, pictures, and graphs*
- *Count with understanding and recognize "how many" in sets of objects*

Math
Charting
Whole number operations
Counting
Equalities and inequalities

Science
Life science
  human senses

Integrated Processes
Observing
Comparing and contrasting
Sorting and classifying
Collecting and recording data
Interpreting data
Communicating

Materials
Color Chart, enlarged
I Can See a Rainbow big book (see *Management 3*)
Colored markers and/or colored pencils
Rainbow Song
Construction paper: red, orange, yellow, green, blue, indigo, violet

Background Information
Teaching the recognition of color is one of the first concepts taught in primary classrooms. Tying color lessons to eyesight seems natural for students. You may find that some students may have difficulty distinguishing between certain colors. For example, shades of red may look orangish to some. Some of the students, especially the boys, may be colorblind or color deficient. Be sensitive to these differences and use the opportunity to explain that we are all unique individuals. Going into the scientific information regarding the reasons for these differences would not be developmentally appropriate at this age. Simply learning that there are differences, or experiencing the differences, is enough.

Management
Prior to class time:
1. The class *Color Chart* will need to be enlarged by using either an enlarging machine or an opaque projector.
2. Teach the students the *Rainbow Song.*
3. Construct a class *I Can See A Rainbow* big book (see instructions). Do not put any objects in the pockets at this time.

Procedure

1. Sing the *Rainbow Song* while flipping through the big book you have made. As you sing the song, flip through to the next color page of the book.
2. Hold up a piece of red construction paper and say the color. Have students look around the room until they find objects that are the same color as the paper. Ask them to name those objects.
3. As red objects are named, the teacher (or a student) will draw these items in the appropriate place on the *Color Chart* using a red marker. Once several items have been recognized, proceed in the same manner with the next colors (orange, yellow, green, blue, indigo and violet) until you have finished all the colors in the *Rainbow Song.*
4. Tell the students that they are going to decide which items to put in the pockets of the class *I Can See A Rainbow* big book. Ask them what object they would like to use to represent red. Fill in the name of the object on the sentence strip at the bottom of the page. For example, I can see a red *apple.* Continue with the other colors.
5. After the students have dictated what to write in the blank spaces, ask them to draw or paint the objects to be put in the pockets. Encourage them to use different mediums such as chalk, felt pen, paint, crayons.
6. Give the students an opportunity to make their own *I Can See A Rainbow* book. There are two different strips provided for the cover of the individual student's *I Can See A Rainbow* book. One has the title *I Can See A Rainbow.* The students then copy this sentence on the blanks below. The second title strip has *I can see a rainbow* _____. The blank line is for the students to either dictate or write in the last part of the sentence. Examples might be: I can see a rainbow in the sky, or between the clouds, or over me. It is suggested that you use one or the other depending on the abilities of your students.

Discussion

1. What colors did our eyes find in the classroom?
2. Let's count all the objects in each color and write the number in each column of our chart.
3. For which color did we have the most objects recorded? How could you tell? How many more ___ _____objects did we see than _____ objects?
4. Which color has the least number of objects recorded?
5. If you close your eyes, can you still see all the colors in our room? What do we need to see things?
6. Did your eyes find colors that are not on the graph? What are they? How can we show them on a chart or graph?

Extensions

1. Have the students bring old magazines from home and cut out pictures of objects. Specify one color each day. Have them glue their pictures to a piece of the same color construction paper. When you are finished with the various colors, staple them all together so each child can have a personal color book.
2. Show the students a prism and point out how a rainbow can be made by shining light through the prism.
3. Talk about how different colors make you feel. What do you think of when you hear about the color green?...red?... blue?, etc.
4. Do the AIMS activity *Reach For A Rainbow* found in *Spring Into Math and Science* that has students graph their favorite color of the rainbow.

Curriculum Correlation

Language Arts:
1. Students will finish the sentence: "Today I found a/an (color word)(object) in our classroom." Have students select the color words from a list of colors put on word strips.
2. Students make their own *I Can See A Rainbow* books to take home.

Literature:
see *Bibliography: Sense of Sight*

Home Links

1. Specify a different color each day. Give the students a piece of paper to take home to draw an object from their home of that color. Have students bring the paper back to school to display on the color wall.
2. Each day have students bring a small item (it must fit into a lunch sack) from home. Ask them to identify the color of the item and to try to find the written word that matches the color of the object.
3. Have students select a color that they should try to wear for the next day. If some students cannot wear the selected colors, have ribbons or pieces of construction paper in the selected color that can be pinned to their shirts.

Color Chart

Red
Orange
Yellow
Green
Blue
Indigo
Violet

I CAN SEE A RAINBOW
Big Book Instructions

1. Cut construction paper to the following sizes to make a big book with a white cover and pages the colors of the rainbow. Because the pages of the book have different dimensions, the book will have a layered look.

   white   12" X 18" (cover)
   red   12" X 12"
   orange   12" X 13"
   yellow   12" X 14"
   green   12" X 15"
   blue   12" X 16"
   indigo   12" X 17"
   violet   12" X 18" (back page)

2. Fold a 3-inch strip up from the bottom of each page to form a pocket. To hold the pocket in place, staple twice along its right side.

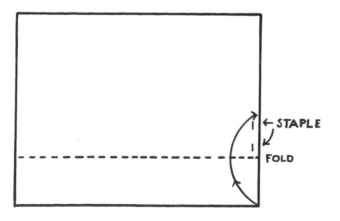

3. Assemble the pages in their proper order. Staple along the left side. Cut a 3" X 12" strip of any color to use for the binding on the left side of the book. Fold it in half as illustrated and glue it to the left side of the book.

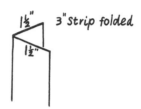

4. Cut out the entire sentence strip if you want your students to copy the text. Cut out just the top script if you want them to read each strip and fill in their own objects. Glue the sentence strips onto each pocket.

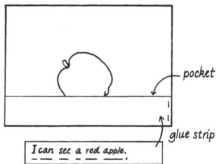

5. Allow students to illustrate different objects that would fit into the pockets. Encourage them to use a variety of mediums: chalk, paint, sponge painting, colored pencils, markers, etc. You may choose to use only one object for each pocket, or you can change the objects each time the book is read.

I can see a red _____ _ _ _ _ _ _ _ _ _ _

I can see an orange _____ _ _ _ _ _ _ _ _ _ _

I can see a yellow _____ _ _ _ _ _ _ _ _ _ _

I can see a green _____

I can see a blue _____

I can see an indigo _____

I can see a rainbow.

I can see a rainbow _____

I can see a violet _____

Rainbow Song

Words by Suzy Gazlay

Tune: Reuben and Rachel
Composer: Unknown

How we love to see a rainbow
Telling us the storm is through,
Made when sunlight shines on raindrops
Here's a rainbow just for you.

Red, the top, the highest color,
Orange, we'll find it just below;
Yellow follows, bright and sunny,
Green, the middle one, we know.

Blue comes next,
like sky in summer;
Indigo, is purple blue;
Violet, is the bottom color;
There's a rainbow just for you!

Topic
Sense of sight

Key Question
How can we use the colors of blue, red, and yellow to make other colors?

Learning Goal
Students will become aware that they use their sense of sight to detect colors.

Guiding Document
Project 2061 Benchmarks
- *People can often learn about things around them by just observing those things carefully, but sometimes they can learn more by doing something to the things and noting what happens.*
- *The brain enables human beings to think and sends messages to other body parts to help them work properly.*
- *People use their senses to find out about their surroundings and themselves. Different senses give different information. Sometimes a person can get different information about the same thing by moving closer to it or further away from it*

Science
Life science
    human senses

Integrated Processes
Observing
Comparing and contrasting
Sorting and classifying
Collecting and recording data
Interpreting data

Materials
For the class:
    Color Frames (see *Management 5*)
    red, yellow, blue colored cellophane
    crayons
    6 c. prepared cake frosting (see *Management 3*)
    paste food coloring (see *Management 3*)
    optional: 2- and 3-part *Color Mixing Palettes*

For each student:
    craft stick

two paper plates
2 Color Combination sheets

Background Information
Teaching the recognition of color is one of the first concepts taught in primary classrooms. Tying color lessons to eyesight seems natural for students. In this activity students will mix the primary colors of pigment (red, blue, and yellow) to produce secondary colors. Their artistic expressions in color should begin to progress as they learn to mix colors to form other colors.

You may find students often perceive colors differently. Some of the students especially boys, may be colorblind or color deficient. Be sensitive to these differences and explain to students that we are all unique individuals. Going into the scientific information regarding the reasons for these differences would not be developmentally appropriate at this age. Simply learning that there are differences, or experiencing the differences, is enough.

Management
1. The activity has students mixing white cake frosting which has been colored red, blue, and yellow to discover the wide range of colors that can be made through combinations.
2. If any of your students are sensitive to sugar, softened cream cheese can be substituted for the cake frosting.
3. Prior to doing this activity, prepare frosting (or cream cheese). You will need a total of six cups of white frosting divided into three, two-cup containers. Using the **paste** food coloring which can be purchased at cake decorating stores or hobby supply stores, color two cups of the frosting red, two cups blue, and two cups yellow. You only need about 1/4 teaspoon of paste food coloring for each container of frosting. Keep containers covered.
4. An assessment of color combinations is built into the lesson in which students use *Color Frames* with cellophane in the three primary colors. The students will determine which colors need to be combined to produce the secondary colors.
5. Copy the *Color Frames* onto card stock and cut out around the outer edge and the inner circle. Cut a piece of cellophane slightly larger than the hole in the frame. Tape the cellophane to the frame. Each

group of students will need three frames: one with red cellophane, one with yellow, and one with blue.

Procedure

1. Prepare one paper plate per student by placing one tablespoon of each of the three colors of frosting (or cream cheese) around the rim of the plate leaving a lot of space between each color.
2. Tell the students that they are going to learn how certain colors are made.
3. Distribute a prepared paper plate and one popsicle stick to each student.
4. Ask the students to identify the colors of frosting on the plates. Tell them that these three colors are called *primary colors* and that they will be used to make other colors.
5. Instruct the students to use their popsicle sticks to carefully separate a small portion of the red frosting and to put it in the middle of the plate. Have them add the same amount of yellow frosting to the red sample and mix the two together. Ask them to identify the color made by mixing red and yellow.
6. Tell the students to lick their popsicle sticks so they do not contaminate the next colors they will mix.
7. Continue this method by mixing blue and yellow to make green, and blue and red to make purple. Review the three primary colors. Ask them to identify the colors made when two primary colors are mixed. Inform them that these new colors are called *secondary colors.*
8. To reinforce the resulting colors distribute one *Color Combination* activity sheet. Have students color the palettes with the primary colors they mixed. The intersection of the two primary colors should produce the secondary color. The top palettes should mix red and yellow, the middle palettes mix blue and yellow, and the bottom palettes mix blue and red.
9. Have students compare and contrast their color combinations and ask if the colors they mixed are all the same. Students will notice that the colors are not the same. Tell them that the color depends on how much of each of the primary colors was mixed. Let the students have some free-exploration time to see what happens when more of one of the primary colors is added to the combination.
10. Distribute a second paper plate to each student. Inform them that they are now going to combine samples of their newly formed secondary colors. Begin by combining equal amounts of orange frosting and green frosting. Continue combining the other secondary colors (green and violet, and violet and orange) from their first plate.

Discussion

1. What color did you make when you mixed red and yellow?
2. Was your neighbor's orange the same? Why or why not? [it had more yellow, or it had more red]
3. How do the paint palettes you colored show the same thing?
4. What colors were made by mixing yellow and blue? What are two ways you could show this to me? [mix the frosting or show you the colored palettes]
5. What happened when we mixed blue and red?
6. The colors that we started with are called *primary colors.* Do you remember which colors these were? [red, blue, yellow]
7. When we mixed two of these primary colors, we formed another color. This new color is called a *secondary color.* What are the secondary colors? [orange, green, violet] Remind students that they can check the *Color Combination* activity sheets they colored.
8. What color did we get when we mixed two secondary colors?
9. Did we all get the same color? Why or why not? [different people used different amounts of colors]
10. Did anyone make black? How did you do it?
11. Why is this lesson valuable?

Assessment

1. Pass out the *Color Frames* to groups of four students. Allow them to mix colors by overlaying the frames one on top of the other to see the resulting combination.
2. Ask them to make violet.
3. Ask them to make green.
4. Ask them to make orange.
5. What is your favorite color and how do you make it?

Extension

1. Enlarge two 3-part *Color Mixing Palettes.* Color to show the combinations of the primary colors. Primary, secondary, and brown will be evident. Ask the students to tell you how the picture shows how orange is made...violet...green...brown.
2. Use the other enlarged 3-part *Color Mixing Palette* to display pictures students have cut from old magazines. Put orange pictures in the intersection of the red and yellow palettes. Place brown pictures in the center showing the combination of the three primary colors. Continue using the same procedure to display pictures depicting the three primary colors, the three secondary colors, and brown.

Curriculum Correlation

Literature:
    see *Bibliography: Sense of Sight*

COLORS

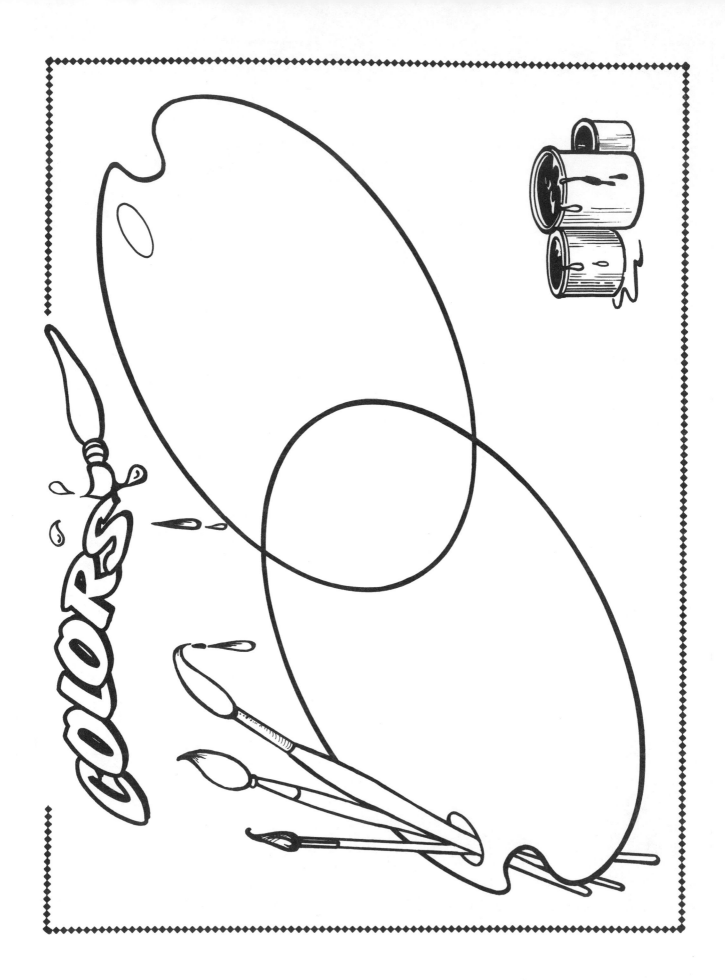

Colors

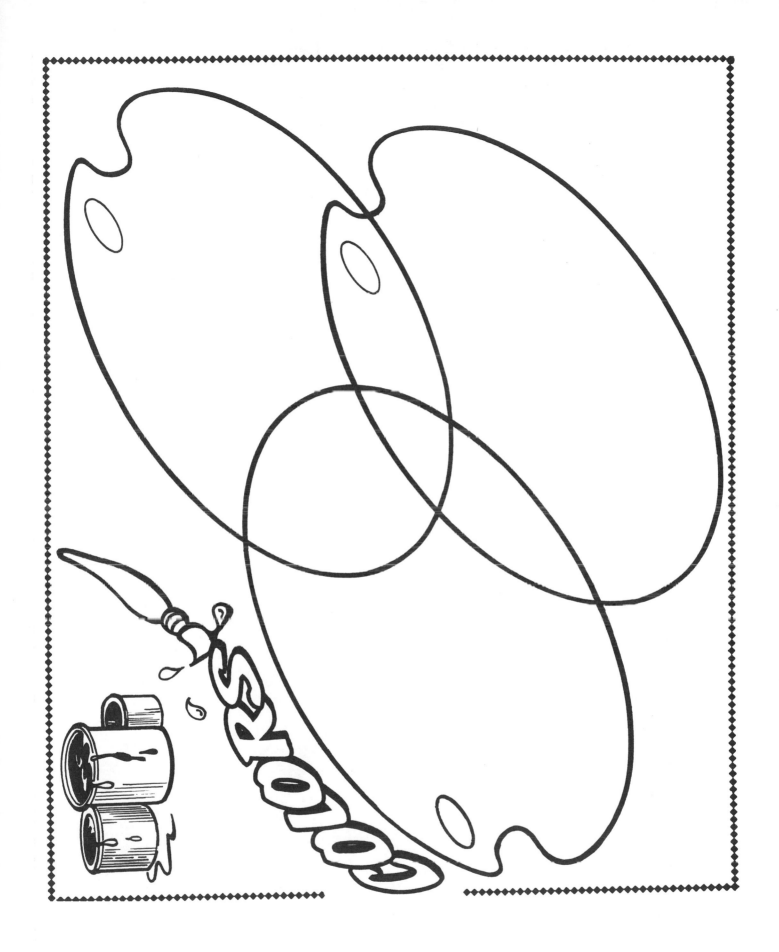

COLOR FRAME

Water Colors

Topic
Sense of sight

Key Question
What does a color wheel show us?

Learning Goal
Students will become aware that they use their sense of sight to detect colors.

Guiding Document
Project 2061 Benchmarks

- *People can often learn about things around them by just observing those things carefully, but sometimes they can learn more by doing something to the things and noting what happens.*
- *The brain enables human beings to think and sends messages to other body parts to help them work properly.*
- *People use their senses to find out about their surroundings and themselves. Different senses give different information. Sometimes a person can get different information about the same thing by moving closer to it or further away from it*

Math
Charting

Science
Life science
  human senses

Integrated Processes
Observing
Comparing and contrasting
Sorting and classifying
Collecting and recording data
Interpreting data
Communicating

Materials
For the class:
  Water Color Wheel (see *Management 1*)
  water
  food coloring: red, yellow, blue

For each group:
  3 plastic cups
  3 drinking straws
  paper towels

For each student:
  waxed paper
  2 *Water Color Wheel* activity pages
  toothpick
  optional: crayons: red, yellow, blue

Background Information
  Teaching the recognition of color is one of the first concepts taught in primary classrooms. Tying color lessons to eyesight seems natural for students. Bringing the color wheel into the lesson further enhances the lesson by reinforcing the connection between primary and secondary colors. The students' artistic expressions in color should begin to progress as they learn to mix colors to form other colors.

  You may find students often perceive colors differently. Some of the students, especially the boys, may be colorblind or color deficient. Be sensitive to these differences and explain to students that we are all unique individuals. Going into the scientific information on the reasons for these differences would not be developmentally appropriate at this age. Simply learning that there are differences, or experiencing the differences, is enough.

Management
1. Enlarge the *Water Color Wheel* by using either an enlarging machine or an opaque projector. Use the appropriate colors to fill in the wedges of the *Water Color Wheel*.
2. Duplicate two copies of the *Water Color Wheel* activity page for each student.
3. This activity should be used as a follow-up to *Color My World*.
4. Put about 50 ml of water into each cup. Add food coloring so that each group will have a cup with red water, a cup with yellow water, and a cup with blue water.
5. Cut straws in half and put two halves in each cup.
6. Tear off waxed paper so each student will have about one square foot.

Procedure
1. Introduce the *Water Color Wheel*. Ask them if they remember how the colors are made. [You begin with the primary colors of red, blue, and yellow. When

you mix two primary colors, you get the secondary colors of violet, orange, and green.]

2. Tell students that they are going to mix colors once again. Make certain each group of students has three cups of colored water with straws, waxed paper, *Water Color Wheel* activity sheets, paper towels, and toothpicks.

3. Direct students to place the waxed paper on top of one of their *Water Color Wheel* activity sheets. Show students how to put the straw into the colored water, squeeze the end of the straw tightly to hold the water in the straw, put the straw over the waxed paper and to release the tight squeeze. Allow time for practice.

4. When students have learned the technique for putting drops of water onto their waxed paper, have them use their paper towels to wipe all the drops off.

5. Have students put a drop the size of a nickel of each of the three primary colors onto their waxed paper. Direct the students to place the appropriate color of water in the specified sections. Ask them to use their toothpicks to pull a little bit of the red drop to the center of the waxed paper. Then have them pull a little of the yellow drop to the center and combine the two. Once orange is formed, have them drag that drop to the section between the red and yellow section labeled *orange* on their color wheel.

6. Continue as above with yellow and blue, forming green, with red and blue, forming violet, etc.

7. Using their second *Water Color Wheel* activity sheet, direct the students to record the colors formed by putting drops of the colored water onto the sheet or using crayons. The dried, colored drops may not be as bright as the colored water, but students can easily distinguish the various colors. Have the students compare their results with the enlarged *Color Wheel* you made.

8. Using the circles at the bottom of the *Water Color Wheel* activity sheet, direct the students to drag opposite colors (complimentary colors) on the color wheel into the circles at the bottom of the page. For example: red and green in the first two circles. Then, as before, direct the students to drag a small portion of the red to the bottom circle, and then a small portion of the green into that same bottom circle. When these colors combine, they will form brown. Note: When you mix opposite colors on the color wheel together you get different shades of browns. The more of one color you mix, the more the shade of brown has of that color. For example, if you mix equal amounts of red and green together, you will get brown; but if you mix more red into the sample, it will create a reddish-brown shade. More green in the mix produces a greenish brown.

9. Instruct the students to record their results, as before, on their second *Water Color Wheel* activity sheet.

Discussion

1. How are our colors different? Are all our oranges the same color of orange? Are all our violets the same color of violet? Are the browns the same or different?

2. How do you think you make the different shades?

3. What colors did you mix together to get brown?

4. Help the students to notice that when you mix red and yellow together, you get orange which is between red and yellow on the color wheel and in the rainbow. When you mix yellow and blue together, you get green which is again between yellow and blue on the color wheel and in the rainbow. Indigo and violet are produced from the mixing of red and blue. Indigo has more blue than does violet. (You may want to have students combine differing amounts of blue and red to see the various colors that are produced.)

Extensions

1. Assist the students in placing colors not found in the rainbow on the enlarged *Color Palettes* from *Color My World*. Discuss with them how these colors are made. [by mixing other colors together]

2. You may want to duplicate the *Color Mixing Palettes Two-Part* activity page that represent more shades of brown. i.e. orange and blue, yellow and violet.

3. Give the students old magazines, scraps of construction paper, and/or paint chip samples which can be obtained from a local paint store. Ask students to find colors to put on the color wheel. You may want to discuss different shades and tints with the students.

4. Have the students bring old magazines from home and cut out pictures of objects. Specify one color each day and glue their pictures to a piece of the same color construction paper. When you are finished with the various colors, staple them all together so each child can have a personal color book.

Water Color Wheel

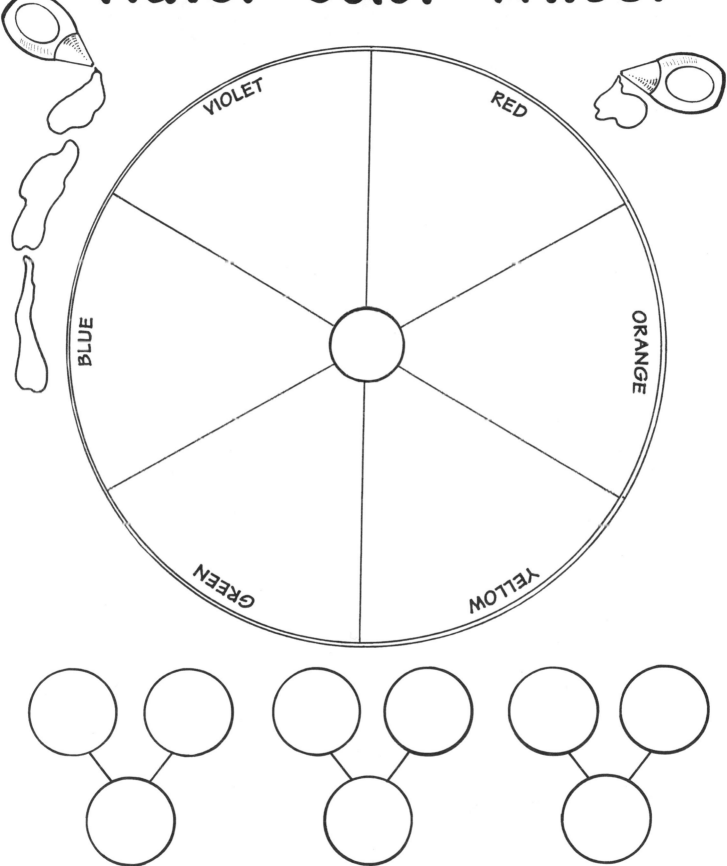

THE EYES HAVE IT

Topic
Animal and human vision

Key Questions
1. What kinds of animals have compound vision?
2. What kinds of animals have telescopic vision?
3. How do the different kinds of eyesight help these animals?

Learning Goal
Students will use models to simulate compound and telescopic vision.

Guiding Document
Project 2061 Benchmarks
- *Some animals and plants are alike in the way they look and in the things they do, and others are very different from one another.*
- *Plants and animals have features that help them live in different environments.*
- *People use their senses to find out about their surroundings and themselves. Different senses give different information. Sometimes a person can get different information about the same thing by moving closer to it or further away from it.*

Science
Life science
   vision

Integrated Processes
Observing
Comparing and contrasting
Sorting and classifying
Collecting and recording data
Interpreting data
Applying

Materials
For the class:
   binoculars
   class graph (see *Management 4*)
   spray adhesive
   transparent tape
   silver mylar
   card stock

For each student:
   magazines (see *Management 2*)
   student journals
   crayons
   scissors
   glue

Background Information
Birds, mammals, insects, fish, and amphibians have developed complex eye structures which give detailed pictures of the world about them. With their telescopic vision, hawks, eagles, and owls can use their keen sight to spot a rabbit hopping through underbrush a thousand feet below them. Compound eyes, found in many insects, are the type most frequently observed in nature. In every case, the way an animal perceives light is dictated by its particular needs; the way it catches food; how it evades its enemies; the way it travels (if it flies, swims, or crawls); and whether it is a diurnal (active during daytime) or nocturnal (active at nighttime) animal.

In this activity the students will use models to simulate two different types of vision in animals: compound and telescopic vision. These models are intended to give students in the primary grades an awareness of the diversity in animal vision. They are not intended as anatomical models.

Management
1. Prepare materials for vision tube prior to class time (see *Make a Vision Tube*). Use spray adhesive to affix mylar to sheets of card stock. Silver mylar often can be purchased in stores which specialize in helium balloons, art supply stores, and hobby/craft shops. Work with small sections (8" x 12") of card stock so the mylar does not wrinkle. Use a paper cutter to make three 1" x 4" pieces of mylar-covered card stock for each student.
2. Each student will need at least three pictures from magazines or other sources of animals with compound and binocular vision.
3. Take the students outdoors during the portion of the activity in which they use binoculars.
4. Use a large piece of butcher paper, plastic table cloth, or similar material to prepare a large two-column floor graph. Use the labels provided in this lesson for naming the sections of the graph: *compound vision* and *telescopic vision*.

5. Prepare the student journals before the activity. Cut and fold the blacklines provided to form a small book.

Procedure
Compound Vision:
1. Make the vision tubes.
2. As students enjoy looking through their vision tubes, discuss what they see and how things look to them.
3. Ask the student to try to imagine what kind of animal would have *compound vision.* [insects] Have students guess how they might change the way they walk and reach for things if they suddenly had compound vision.
4. Instruct the students to put one finger into the front opening of the vision tube and to look at it through the other end.
5. Point out that they are looking at only one finger, yet they see many images of that finger.

6. Discuss the fact that the eyes of an insect do not work the same way in which the mirrors are working; however, the insect does see multiple images of the one object on which it is focusing. Point out that the insect does not see the image as clearly as the students are seeing through the vision tube. Insects see a fuzzy image that is broken up into many parts.

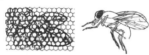

Telescopic Vision:
7. Take students outside. Locate a distant object such as the flag pole.
8. Have students first look at the object with their eyes and discuss how far away it might be. Have them look through the binoculars and notice how close it now looks. (Be sure students are looking through the small lens and not the large.
9. Try to imagine what kind of animal would have this kind of vision. After some discussion, tell them that this is called *telescopic vision* and that birds of prey most commonly have this type of vision. Discuss why they need this type of vision.

Culmination:
10. Instruct students to search for pictures of animals with compound and telescopic vision in magazines or other available resources.

11. Allow the students to sort and graph the magazine pictures as to the different types of vision. Use the large graphing labels and title provided on a two-column floor graph.
12. To use as an assessment or as a culminating activity, allow the students to record in their student journals, samples of the different types of vision studied. They could cut and paste additional pictures from magazines, draw pictures to represent animals, or write the names of animals with the different types of vision on the appropriate pages in their journal.

Discussion
1. Why do some animals have different vision than humans?
2. How does *compound vision* and *telescopic vision* help the different animals? How do you think our lives would be different if we had *compound vision*?...*telescopic vision*?
3. Why don't humans have these types of vision?
4. In what type of habitat does an insect live? How does its eyesight help it to survive?
5. Compare the differences between the eyes of an animal with *compound vision* and those of an animal with *telescopic vision.*
6. If eagles had *compound vision*, how might it change the way they hunt?

Extensions
1. Show a movie of a bird of prey flying high in the sky and then quickly swooping down to catch its prey. Point out that the bird could see its prey from far away in the sky.
2. Show detailed pictures of insects, birds of prey, etc., to more closely examine their eyes.(*National Geographic, Your Big Backyard* magazine is a good resource for these pictures.)
3. Use a microscope to look at the eye of bees, grasshoppers, etc.

Curriculum Correlation
Literature:
    see *Bibliography: Sense of Sight*

Home Link
1. Instruct the students to take their kaleidoscopes on a walk through their neighborhood to see the world with an insect's perspective. Have them walk through their house with the kaleidoscopes and discuss with their families how their life would be different if they saw things with this type of vision.
2. Direct the students to ask their families if they have binoculars at home. Ask them to discuss with their families how they use these and to report back to class.

Animal Vision

In the animal kingdom, there are many different types of eyes, each adapted to the particular needs of the creature. For nearly all animals, vision is a means of survival. Vision is an instrument for gathering food and for safeguarding their lives.

Compound Vision

There are more animals with compound eyes in nature than any other type of eyes. Many insects, crabs, shrimp, and other marine animals have this type of vision.

Compound eyes are composed of multiple light-sensitive units which are joined together. Depending on the animal, one compound eye may contain anywhere from 10 to 30,000 sections.

A component of a compound eye has a lens which is attached to a long-pointed tube. Each lens picks up only a tiny portion of an image. A mosaic-like picture is formed from the combination of all the tiny image portions from the numerous lenses. The tube ends to which the lenses are attached fan out slightly giving the animal a wide field of vision.

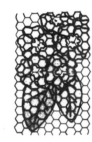

The lenses of the compound eye do not move and, as a result, they cannot produce sharply focused images. The eyes, however, are very good at detecting movement which enables the animal to protect itself and to detect the movement of its food source.

Compound eyes are proportionally larger than our eyes. If we had eyes on the same scale as a dragonfly, our eyes would be about one meter in diameter!

Telescopic Vision

Birds of prey hunt by sight; they have the keenest vision of any animal. They see the world about them much more clearly than the sharpest human eyes. Their extraordinary eyes have two spots on the retina where they can see very clearly: one spot allows for clear sideways vision and the other for clear forward vision.

Proportionally, animals with telescopic vision have huge eyes, as large as the eyes of a human in some cases, though, of course, their heads are much smaller. The eyes of these birds of prey may outweigh their brains!

It is thought that the vision of some eagles may be up to seven times as acute as human eyesight. Observers have claimed that a soaring golden eagle can see a ground squirrel from 1,000 feet in the air. We humans would struggle to see so small an animal at that distance even with binoculars!

Make a Vision Tube

Materials:

- 3-1"x4" pieces of card stock backed with silver mylar
- transparent tape

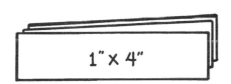

1" x 4"

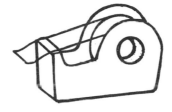

Procedure:

1. Join the 3 pieces of mirrored card stock with tape as sown.

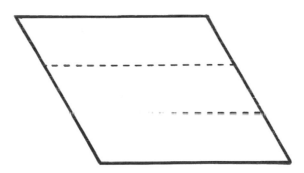

2. Fold the card stock so that the mirrored sides face inward. Tape the third side to the first to form a triangular prism.

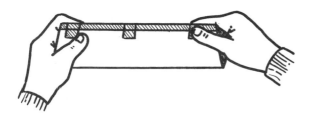

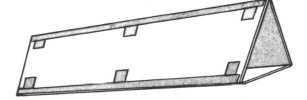

Animal Vision

Science Journal

telescopic vision

I can see _____

compound vision

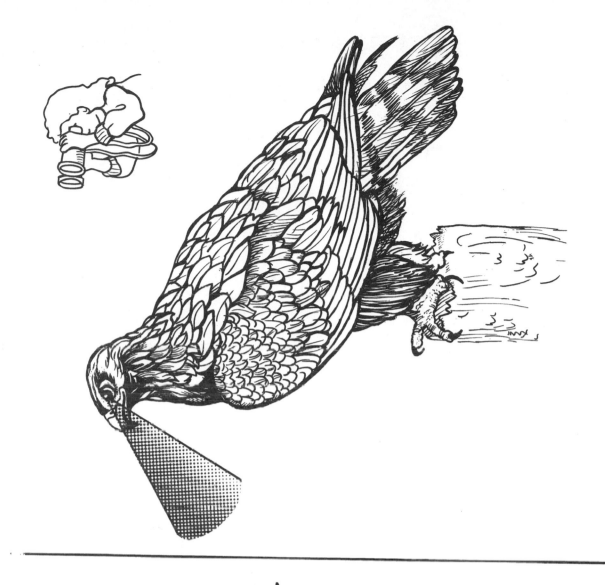

binocular vision

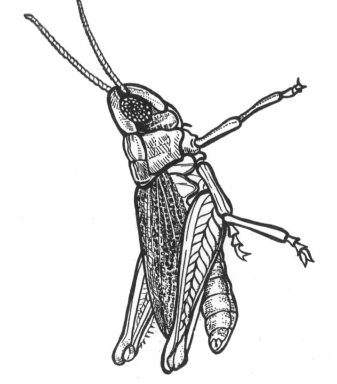

compound vision

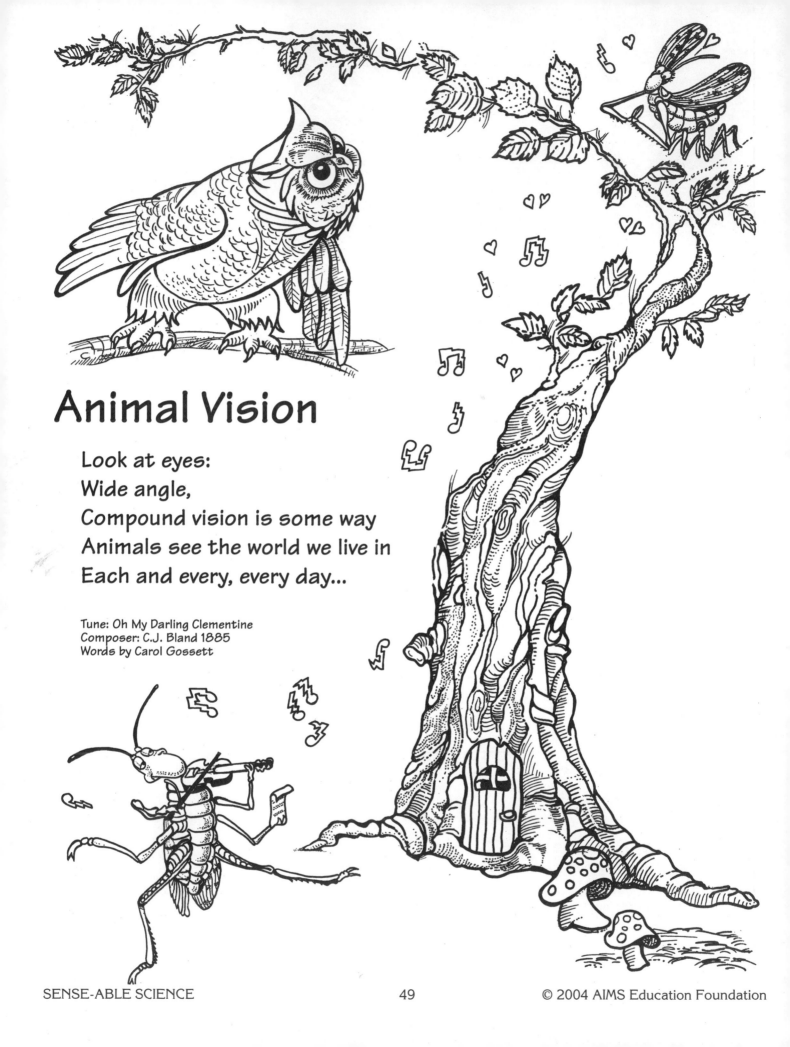

Animal Vision

Look at eyes:
Wide angle,
Compound vision is some way
Animals see the world we live in
Each and every, every day...

Tune: Oh My Darling Clementine
Composer: C.J. Bland 1885
Words by Carol Gossett

Touch

Imagine brushing a feather across the tip of your nose or picking up a hot dish or getting slapped by a twig while walking in the woods. All these imagined events conger up memories which are associated with the sense of touch.

The sense of touch does not come from one specific location on the body. Your skin is studded with thousands of receptors that detect temperature, pressure, and pain. When contact is made with one of the receptors, messages called nerve impulses are sent along nerves to the brain. The brain receives the impulses and commands your body to respond. Over a period of time, some sense receptors may adapt to a certain feel so you no longer notice it.

Some areas of your body perceive touch more than others. The feather may tickle the end of your nose or your lips, but may not tickle

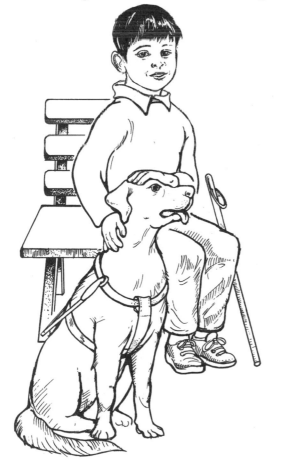

your shoulders. The density of the receptors in your skin varies tremendously over the surface of your body. A square centimeter area on your fingertip may have dozens of skin receptors, while the same sized area on your back may have fewer than one.

Your skin provides a boundary between you and the external world. It is the largest sensory organ of your body. If you are a typical adult, your skin weighs about nine pounds and has a surface area of about 20 square feet.

Down Wave the Waves Begin

Brenda Dahl

We came to stay down at the beach,
My family and I,
To walk along its sandy shores
Beneath its brilliant sky.

The sand is gritty, damp and cold
Down where the waves begin;
I run to meet them as they come
And run away again.

And when I'm not quite fast enough,
They slap and sting and fizz;
I feel the wet sand slip away.
How interesting that is.

From all this sun and wind and play
My cheeks are hot and red.
"Enough of the outdoors for you,"
Is what my father said.

He scooped me up, and bundled me
Inside a rough, dry towel,
Then gathered all my playthings:
My pail, sea shells and trowel.

Into the tub with you, my dear,
Clean clothes are on the shelf.
"There's nothing but pajamas here,"
I mutter to myself.

Then once I'm in the bathtub
With sand and ocean washed away,
As bubbles pop and tickle me,
It's where I want to stay.

But the last thing I remember
As I slip into my bed,
Is just how soft my pillow feels
Beneath my heavy head.

Sense of Touch
A Rap

How <u>much</u> can I <u>touch</u>,
Can I <u>touch</u> with my <u>fingers</u>?
I can <u>touch</u> my knees and <u>ankles</u>,
I can <u>touch my toes</u>;
I can <u>touch</u> my <u>elbows</u>,
I can <u>touch</u> my head and <u>shoulders</u>;
I can <u>touch</u> my <u>middle</u>,
I can <u>touch</u> my nose.

I touch <u>furry</u>, I touch <u>fuzzy</u>,
I touch <u>soft</u> or rough or <u>pointed</u>,
I touch <u>slimy</u>, I touch <u>gooey</u>,
I touch <u>sand and dirt</u>.
I touch <u>cold</u>, I touch <u>warm</u>,
Not too <u>hot</u>—my touch will <u>warn</u> me—
It's a <u>way</u> that touch <u>protects</u> me
So <u>I don't get</u> hurt.

It's <u>funny</u> how my <u>brain</u>
Is con<u>nected</u> to my <u>fingers</u>,
'Cause no <u>matter</u> what I'm <u>touching</u>,
My <u>brain can tell</u>.
And I <u>know</u> they are con<u>nected</u>,
'Cause my <u>skin</u> and brain to<u>gether</u>
Let me <u>feel</u> the world <u>around</u> me,
And they <u>really</u> do it <u>well</u>! . . .

written by Suzy Gazlay

•**Words and parts of words that
are underlined indicate need for a
heavier accent in your voice.**

Shape Search

Topic
Sense of touch

Key Question
How can you sort and classify shapes without using your eyes?

Learning Goals
Students will:
1. sort and match shapes using their sense of touch; and
2. sort and describe shapes according to attributes such as number of sides and number of corners.

Guiding Documents
Project 2061 Benchmarks
- *People use their senses to find out about their surroundings and themselves. Different senses give different information. Sometimes a person can get different information about the same thing by moving closer to it or further away from it*
- *Describing things as accurately as possible is important in science because it enables people to compare their observations with those of others.*
- *Numbers and shapes can be used to tell about things.*

NCTM Standards 2000*
- *Recognize, name, build, draw, compare, and sort two- and three-dimensional shapes*
- *Describe attributes and parts of two- and three-dimensional shapes*
- *Create mental images of geometric shapes using spatial memory and spatial visualization*

Math
Geometry
two-dimensional shape recognition

Science
Life science
human senses

Integrated Processes
Observing
Comparing and contrasting
Sorting and classifying
Predicting
Organizing

Generalizing
Making and testing hypotheses

Materials
For making card sets:
sandpaper
glue
64 cards, 3 x 5 inches

For each student:
personal blindfold (see *Appendix: Science Tools*)
8 pieces of construction paper (12 x 18 inches)
colored tape, optional
student recording page

Background Information
We use information from previous experiences to help us understand our world and to learn about new things. Much of the information is gathered through the use of our five senses. In this activity, students will try to determine four different sandpaper shapes by using only their sense of touch. They will use their prior knowledge of shapes and the sensory input from touch to determine the shapes.

Management
1. Prior experience with pattern blocks or shapes in general is suggested before beginning this lesson.
2. To prevent the spread of any eye conditions from one child to another, it is advised that students make their own personal blindfolds. This should be done prior to the beginning of this activity. The blindfolds may be used for other activities.
3. Cut out the following shapes from sandpaper and glue onto the 3" X 5" cards: *large triangle, small triangle, large square, small square, large circle, small circle, large rectangle,* and *small rectangle.* Make eight sets of these cards.
4. Make eight sorting mats using 12" X 18" pieces of construction paper. Divide the construction paper into four sections as in *Figure 1.* You may want to put colored tape over the lines dividing the sections so students can determine their borders when

blind folded. Cut out the *Shapes...Sorting Mat* from sandpaper. Glue one shape in the upper left corner of each section of the paper to match the sequence on the student's recording sheet.

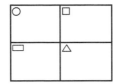

Figure 1

5. Set up one station with eight sets of cards and eight sorting mats.
6. A cross-age tutor or adult aide is helpful in directing the search for shapes.

Procedure

1. As a whole class activity, show students the cards with the shapes on them. Ask them what they see. Ask them how they knew what the shapes were. What part of their bodies did they use in determining the shapes? [looked at them, eyes]
2. Ask students what part of their bodies they would use to tell what the shapes were if they could not use their eyes.
3. With the students, develop a hypothesis as to how well the children will be able to determine the shapes with and without using their eyes. [If I can see the shapes, I will be able to classify all of them. If I cannot see the shapes, I will be able to touch them and classify the circles and triangles.]
4. Using the sense of sight, have one student classify the shape cards onto a sorting mat. Ask the students if this was a difficult task. Why or why not? Check the hypothesis. Was it confirmed?
5. Tell the students they will each have a turn to go to the station and with a blindfold over their eyes, they will classify the shape cards by placing them in the appropriate sections of their sorting mats.
6. Organize students into groups of eight. Ask them to bring their personal blindfolds to the station when it is their turn. Allow one group to work at the station at a time.
7. While blindfolded, let each student feel the shape on each card and put it into the appropriate section of his or her sorting mat.
8. After students have finished, have them remove the blindfolds and draw their results on the student recording sheet *Feel and Find*. Students will draw the shapes they classified in each section, whether right or wrong.

Discussion

1. Were there any errors in classifying the shapes? Which shape was the easiest to classify? Why? Which shape was the most difficult? Why?
2. Reread the class hypotheses. Compare (look at similarities) and contrast (look at differences) the hypotheses to the students' experiences with the activity. Can we support our hypotheses?

3. Is there a time we use only one sense by itself? Explain.
4. Are there any students that do not have the use of one or more of their senses? How does this affect what they know or how they learn about their world?

Extensions

1. While the students are blindfolded, direct them to make a pattern with the cards. [circle, square, circle, square. . .circle, square, rectangle, circle, square, rectangle. . .]
2. While the students are blindfolded, let them feel an object such as a block, ball, or eraser, and determine what it is.
3. Talk about physical handicaps and how they affect a person's life.
4. Add a third-sized shape to introduce the terms *big, bigger, biggest* or *small, smaller, smallest*. Repeat the activity, sorting by size instead of shape. Find the biggest circle, the smallest square. Which of these two shapes is bigger? How can you tell?

Curriculum Correlation

Social Studies:
1. What shapes are in our room?
2. Of which shape is there the most?

Art:
1. Draw pictures using shapes.
2. Cut and paste pictures using only shapes cut out of textured wallpaper.

Language Arts:
Use story *Changes, Changes* by Pat Hutchins. Macmillan Publishing, 1971. How did the family use shapes? What could they build out of shapes?

Science:
Take a nature walk around school. Look for shapes in nature.

Home Links

1. Give students a homework paper like the sorting mat. Have them draw something in each section from their home that they could tell the shape of by touching it. A square table would be acceptable, but squares on nontextured wallpaper would not be acceptable because students would need their eyes to determine the shape.
2. Have each student share an object that is one of the four shapes studied in this lesson. Set it at the station for students to touch.
3. Have students bring a picture of an object with one of the shapes and paste it on a large class poster which has been divided into sections like the sorting mat.

* Reprinted with permission from *Principles and Standards for School Mathematics*, 2000 by the National Council of Teachers of Mathematics. All rights reserved.

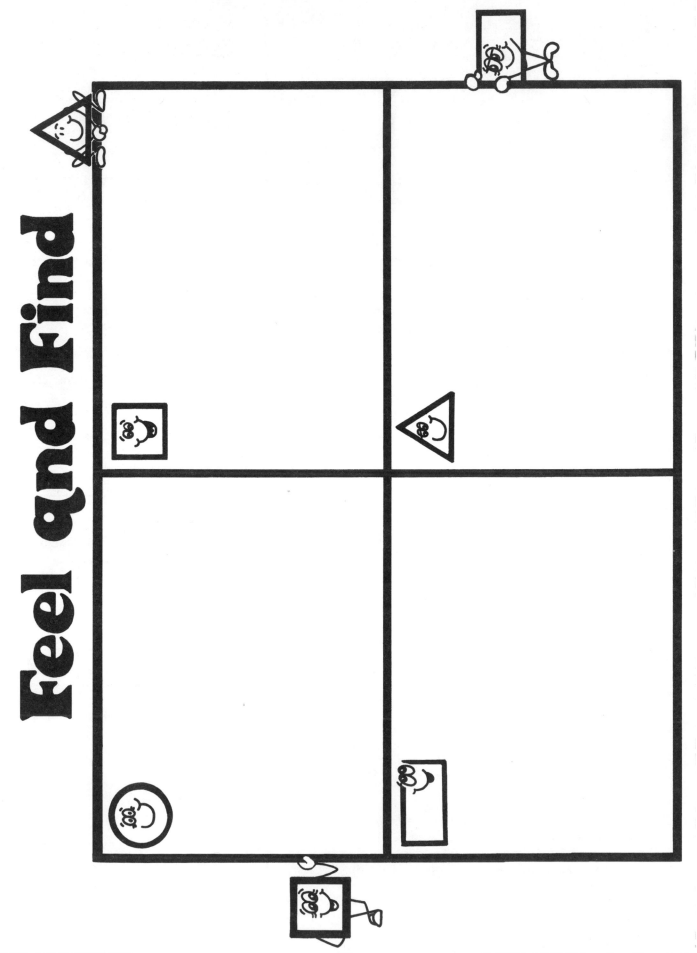

Feel and Find

Shapes...

Shapes... Sorting Mat

Card Set

Touch and Tell

Topic
Sense of touch

Key Question
How can you match the textures of pieces of fabric without seeing them?

Learning Goal
Students will identify and classify rough and smooth textures by using the sense of touch.

Guiding Documents
Project 2061 Benchmarks
- *People use their senses to find out about their surroundings and themselves. Different senses give different information. Sometimes a person can get different information about the same thing by moving closer to it or further away from it*
- *Describing things as accurately as possible is important in science because it enables people to compare their observations with those of others.*

NCTM Standards 2000*
- *Count with understanding and recognize "how many" in sets of objects*
- *Sort and classify objects according to their attributes and organize data about the objects*
- *Represent data using concrete objects, pictures, and graphs*

Math
Graphing
Number sense and numeration
Tallying

Science
Life science
human senses

Integrated Processes
Observing
Comparing and contrasting
Sorting and classifying
Predicting
Recording data
Interpreting data
Communicating

Materials
1 2-lb. empty coffee can or a large wide-mouthed

Plastic jar
1 adult-size tube sock
Nylon filament tape (shipping tape)
Patterned adhesive-back paper, optional
20 or more pieces of 3 x 3-inch fabric swatches (see *Management 3*)
Glue
Scissors
Tally sheet, one per student
Sorting sheet (see *Management 4*)

Background Information
The sense of touch is not highly developed in young children. In an attempt to further develop this sense, the teacher is encouraged to explore many experiences that use the sense of touch. In order for children to verbalize about what they are touching, it is first necessary to define the terms of classification. Because these terms are relative, it is often difficult for students to apply them to various objects. This activity has students classify fabric swatches as rough or smooth. A beginning definition for rough may be having a bumpy-type surface like the feel of carpet or sandpaper. Smooth things have a slick-type surface like a mirror or the glass on the overhead projector. The teacher may wish to do a series of introductory lessons classifying items in the classroom into rough and smooth categories. Once the categories have been defined and experienced, this lesson can be utilized.

Management
1. Prepare the *Touch and Tell* can:
   - Cut off the toe end of the sock so that a 12-inch long section is left
   - Stretch the cut end over top of the can down about one inch and secure with the tape
   - If desired, cover the can with adhesive-backed paper

2. Suggested types of fabrics: velvet, burlap, dotted swiss, linen, cotton, satin, silk, nylon netting
3. To prepare the touch cards:
   - cut fabric swatches into 3" x 3" pieces (10 pairs)
   - glue fabric swatches to the squares of tagboard. (A minimum of 10 sets is suggested).
4. Duplicate one sorting sheet for use at the *Touch and Tell* center for the students to sort and classify their "textured pairs" (the matching fabric swatch cards).To make reusable, copy the sorting sheet on construction paper or tagboard and laminate.
5. This activity can be done as a learning station activity, with groups of 8-10 students exploring the various textures.
6. Copy one tally sheet per student.

Procedure
Opening Discussion:
1. Show the *Touch and Tell* can to the children. Explain that they will be using their sense of touch to find textures that are the same and they will then place the "textured pairs" in either the *smooth or rough* categories on the sorting sheet.
2. Hold up the sorting sheet and have the students review what *smooth* and *rough* mean by locating several objects in the room that would represent smooth and rough.
3. How can we use the sense of touch to find textures that are the same?
4. What do we use when we touch something?

Activity
5. Encourage the students to touch fabric squares which are randomly placed on the floor in front of the small group.
6. Choose one student to reach inside the *Touch and Tell* can and through the sense of touch determine which fabric square displayed on the floor would be a match to the one in the can. Direct the student to point to the square that he/she predicts is a match before pulling the square out of the can.
7. As each pair is found, have the students place the fabric pair in the appropriate category on the sheet.
8. Direct all the students to take turns using the *Touch and Tell* can until all pairs are matched.
9. Using the student tally sheets, tally to find out which category has the most/least.

Discussion
1. What sense did we use today to find the matching pairs?
2. If you had a difficult time sorting the squares, what other sense would make the task easier?
3. What group, smooth or rough, had the most fabric pieces?
4. When you think of smooth things, what do you think of?
5. What things can you name that are rough?

6. Look closely at the rough fabrics; how are they alike? How are they different from any of the smooth fabrics. What does this have to do with making them smooth or rough?
7. Explain why you can use just your sense of touch to sort the squares into rough or smooth.
8. Explain why you cannot use just your sense of touch to sort the squares by color.
9. Using your tally sheets, tell me how many things that you touched were rough?...smooth?

Extensions
1. Add other swatches and repeat the activity.
2. Use pairs of similar shaped objects and challenge the students to match pairs by touch.
3. Have students classify the objects in their backpacks into smooth and rough categories.
4. Change the categories from smooth and rough to hard and soft.
5. Rearrange the fabric squares into different attributes, i.e. color, pattern design, etc. Would the rules about matching our squares need to change? Could we sort with only our sense of touch?
6. Begin a classroom rock collection for purposes of sorting and classifying. Begin with smooth and rough and then substitute attributes such as shiny, dull, speckled, striped, etc.

Curriculum Correlation
Language Arts:
   Make a *Things That Are Rough and Things That Are Smooth* book for your classroom library. Have each student draw an illustration for each category and share it with classmates before putting it into the book.

Literature:
   see *Bibliography: Sense of Touch*

Home Link
1. Send a homework assignment with the children in your class involving the collecting and recording of three objects which would fit into each category.
2. Encourage the parent/child to send real objects for a "Texture Sharing Day." Emphasize only the two textures discussed, and tally
   a. total number of objects brought from home
   b. total number of smooth-textured objects
   c. total number of rough-textured objects

*   Reprinted with permission from *Principles and Standards for School Mathematics*, 2000 by the National Council of Teachers of Mathematics. All rights reserved.

Touch and Tell

s-m-o-o-t-h

rough

Touch and Tell
Tally Sheet

s-m-oo-t-h rough

s-m-oo-t-h rough

s-m-oo-t-h rough

s-m-oo-t-h rough

60

Texture Rough

Texture Smooth

Topic
Sense of touch

Key Question
What sense do we use to decide if something is smooth or rough?

Learning Goal
Students will use their sense of touch to sort and classify objects by texture.

Guiding Documents
Project 2061 Benchmarks
- *People use their senses to find out about their surroundings and themselves. Different senses give different information. Sometimes a person can get different information about the same thing by moving closer to it or further away from it*
- *Describing things as accurately as possible is important in science because it enables people to compare their observations with those of others.*

NCTM Standards 2000*
- *Count with understanding and recognize "how many" in sets of objects*
- *Sort and classify objects according to their attributes and organize data about the objects*
- *Represent data using concrete objects, pictures, and graphs*

Math
Number sense and numeration
Ordering

Science
Life science
   human senses

Integrated Processes
Observing
Comparing and contrasting
Sorting and classifying
Predicting
Collecting and recording data
Interpreting data

Materials
Various objects with distinctive textures (see *Management 6*)
Chart paper or butcher paper
Newsprint (see *Management 3*)
Old crayons
Texture samples for student books (see *Management 6*)
Wheel Books copied on tagboard

Background Information
Touch gives people information about objects in the world around them. Size, shape, and texture are characteristics which can be sensed through touch. Nerve endings in the skin called sense receptors allow people to receive the sensations. These sense receptors are found in all three layers of the skin. The receptors send messages about what is felt through nerve impulses, by way of the nervous system, to the brain.
Terms defined:
Texture — the characteristic structure of a surface.
Rough — A surface that is uneven as a result of projections, irregularities, or breaks.
Smooth — A surface that is free from projections and irregularities

Management
1. Students can work on sorting different objects individually or within small groups after some discussion about *texture* and the terms *rough* and *smooth*.
2. Keep the students focused on the qualities of roughness and smoothness during this investigation. Later, other classifications may be added.
3. The procedures for rubbings should first be modeled by an adult and then supervised briefly to ensure understanding of the process. Newsprint needs to be placed over the object of the rubbing. Remove the paper from an old crayon and, using its broad side, rub it sideways several times over the object until the imprint of the object appears. While rubbing with one hand, it may be necessary to keep the other hand on top of the paper and object so they do not move. Students may need to practice this several times with different objects before getting a satisfactory rubbing. The students may want to create a picture or collage of the rubbings.

4. Make a class chart or a class mural for recording objects found in the room by the students.
5. Copy the student *Wheel Books* onto tagboard and either assemble before class or have them ready in a station for the students to assemble.
6. You will need a collection of several texture samples for the students to glue onto their wheel for their books. Suggested items are: corrugated cardboard, Velcro, plastic wrap, waxed paper, velvet, leaf, corduroy, sandpaper, etc.

Procedure
1. Set out objects with rough or smooth textures. Let students verbalize how the objects feel. Guide them to concluding that all things have texture. Lead them into sorting these objects into categories of *rough* and *smooth*.
2. Encourage students to find other objects in the room which they predict would fit into the categories of *rough* and *smooth*. Students are not to feel these objects before predicting.
3. Record predictions on chart paper.
4. Collect the classroom objects found by the students and ask the students to feel the surfaces. Compare and contrast the actual results with those predicted.
5. Go out-of-doors and repeat this activity finding various objects with smooth or rough characteristics.
6. Have students select an object to make a rubbing on a piece of newsprint (see *Management*).
7. Gather several objects the students have col-lected and arrange them from the roughest to the smoothest.
8. Have the students make a *Texture Rough, Texture Smooth Wheel Book*.

Discussion
1. How do the objects feel? What words describe their textures?
2. How are the objects the same? How are they differen?
3. Are some objects rougher or smoother than others? How can you tell?
4. Can you tell the texture of objects by looking at them? Explain.
5. How many rough objects did we find? How many smooth objects?
6. Did we find more rough or more smooth objects? How could you tell?

Extensions
1. Choose different texture characteristics to observe and record.
2. Use different parts of the body [feet, hair, skin] to decide their textures.

Curriculum Correlation
Literature:
1. Moncure, Jane Belk. *The Touch Book*. Childrens Press. Chicago. 1982.
2. see *Bibliography: Sense of Touch*.

Art:
1. Take newsprint and crayons with you on a nature walk. Make rubbings of various things along the walk.
2. Have students create texture collages using samples from old wallpaper books or fabrics.
3. Have students write about their favorite toys and how they feel.
4. Make a class book of favorite things to touch.

Math:
1. Make texture patterns [rough, rough, smooth (AAB)]
2. Count things in an area of the room or on the playground that are smooth   rough. Tally the findings.
3. Create Venn diagrams for items that may have both rough and smooth textures.

Home Links
1. Ask students to bring a collection of rubbings from home
2. Have students sort objects at home into *rough* and *smooth* and ask an adult to help record the data.

*   Reprinted with permission from *Principles and Standards for School Mathematics*, 2000 by the National Council of Teachers of Mathematics. All rights reserved.

Texture Rough, Texture Smooth
Wheel Book

Materials

For each student booklet:
   one wheel and cover, copied on tag or card stock
   one 5 1/2" x 8" piece of card stock
   various materials with rough and smooth textures
   paper fastener
   tape
   glue
   scissors

Procedure

1. Instruct students to cut around the dark edge of the wheel.

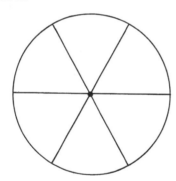

2. Direct the students to choose three objects that are rough and three objects that are smooth. Tell them to glue each of these objects in the sections of the wheel, using one object per section.

3. Tell the students to cut out the front cover along the outer edge. Instruct them to cut out the triangular section to make a "peep hole." (The teacher may need to do this!) This is the front of the wheel holder.

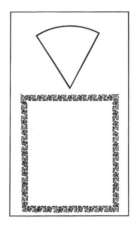

4. Join the front to the back (the plain piece of card stock) by taping along the left side.

5. Using the paper fastener, attach the wheel to the inside of the back of the wheel holder.

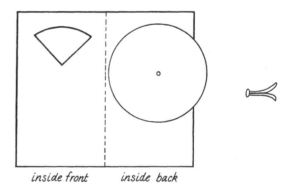

inside front   inside back

6. Glue the top and bottom inside edges of the wheel holder, leaving the wheel free to turn.

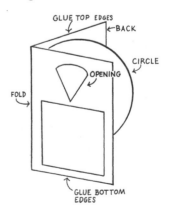

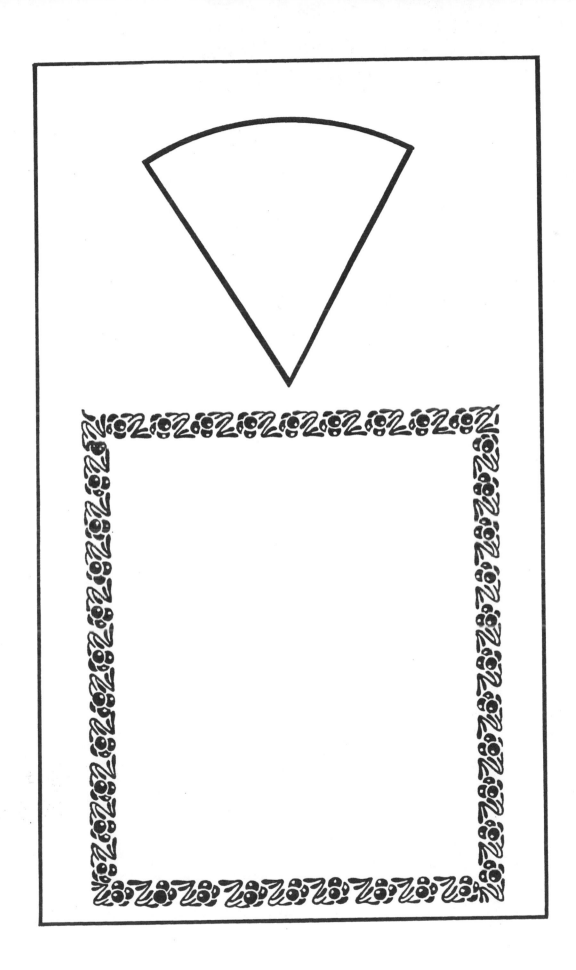

Texture Texture
Rough Smooth

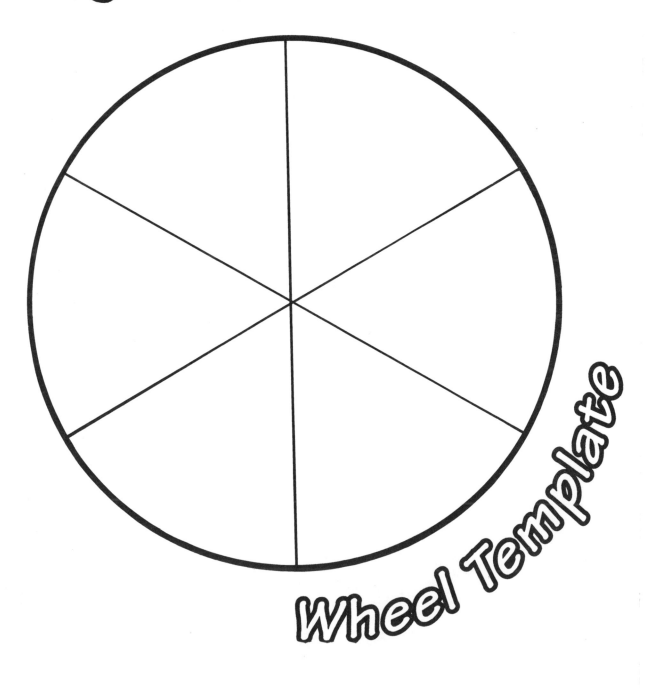

Wheel Template

Kid Gloves

Topic
Senses of touch and sight

Key Question
What senses do you use when you pick up an object?

Learning Goal
Students will gain an understanding of how important the senses of touch and sight are to the understanding of our world.

Guiding Documents
Project 2061 Benchmarks
- *People use their senses to find out about their surroundings and themselves. Different senses give different information. Sometimes a person can get different information about the same thing by moving closer to it or further away from it*
- *Describing things as accurately as possible is important in science because it enables people to compare their observations with those of others.*

NCTM Standards 2000*
- *Count with understanding and recognize "how many" in sets of objects*
- *Sort and classify objects according to their attributes and organize data about the objects*
- *Represent data using concrete objects, pictures, and graphs*

Math
Number sense and numeration
Graphing

Science
Life science
    human senses

Integrated Processes
Observing
Comparing and contrasting
Predicting
Collecting and organizing data
Interpreting data

Materials
For the class:
    chart paper

For each group:
    one pair of women's heavy-duty work gloves
    or child's size knitted gloves
    10 cotton balls (see *Management 1*)

For each student:
    crayons
    personal blindfold (see *Appendix: Science Tools*)
    student journal (see *Management 4*)
    Kid Glove graph

Background Information
Students will realize the value of their sense of touch by diminishing that sense by wearing gloves. To further mask the ability to feel, you must also take away sight with the use of a blindfold so that the students may not see what they are trying to pick up. This activity demonstrates to the students how their sense of touch helps them interact with their environment through picking objects up.

Management
1. Set up a station with a pair of gloves and 10 cotton balls. Use inexpensive cotton balls! They will be harder for students to feel.
2. If students do not have personal blindfolds, make these prior to doing the activity (see *Appendix: Science Tools*).
3. Students will work in a small group at this station while other groups are involved at other stations such as a listening station, library station, manipulative station, etc. An adult helper or cross-age tutor is needed for this activity.
4. Copy and construct student journals prior to classtime. To construct the journal, cut along the solid lines and fold along the broken lines. The page, *My Own Journal,* is the cover page. *Prediction* is to be glued to the back of the cover page, while *Actual* will be glued to the back of the back cover (*How many cotton balls did I pick up?*).

Procedure

1. Ask students if they have ever tried to find anything in the dark? Have them describe their techniques for doing this. [feel the wall to find the light switch; walk with hands outstretched to find the door; shuffle feet to find slippers or shoes]
2. Show the students a cotton ball. Discuss its attributes. Ask them if it would be difficult to pick it up. Give students some free exploration time holding cotton balls, picking them up, and setting them down.
3. Discuss what senses they would use to pick up the cotton ball.
4. Tell students they are going to form a hypothesis about picking up ten cotton balls. Write on chart paper and say, "If I can see and feel the cotton balls, I will be able to pick up _____." (Most students will say all 10.)
5. Ask two or three students to test the hypothesis for the class. Have them show the rest of the class that if they use their senses of sight and touch, they can pick up all ten cotton balls.
6. Tell students that they are going to see what happens when they don't use their senses of sight and touch. Ask them what they could do so they don't use their sense of sight. [wear a blindfold, close our eyes]
7. Inform students that they will form a hypothesis about not being able to see the cotton balls. "If I cannot see the cotton balls, I will be able to pick up ___." Distribute the *Kid Gloves* graphs. Have students draw enough cotton balls to represent their prediction of the number (out of 10) they think they can pick up while wearing a blindfold. Students will test this hypothesis at the center.
8. Ask students what would happen if they couldn't see and couldn't feel the cotton balls? Have the students discuss what they could do so that they don't use their sense of touch, but still pick up the cotton balls. Lead them to conclude that if they wore heavy gloves they couldn't feel the cotton balls.
9. Have them form a hypothesis about how many cotton balls (out of 10) they could pick up without seeing or feeling them and draw their predictions in the appropriate place on the graph.
10. Divide students into groups. One group will go to the *Kid Gloves* station while the others will go to other stations.
11. Have students at the station count the cotton balls to confirm that there are ten. Ask them to state their predictions as a hypothesis. [If I cannot see the cotton balls, I will be able to pick up ___.] One at a time have students put on their blindfolds to test the hypothesis.
12. After determining how many cotton balls were picked up, have each student draw in cotton balls to represent the actual results on the graph.
13. Remind students of the other hypothesis they formed about not being able to see or feel.

[If I cannot see or feel the cotton balls, I can pick up ___.]

14. Students will test this hypothesis by wearing their blindfolds and gloves. After they have performed the test, direct them to record the actual results on their graphs. Also have them record their predictions and actual results in the student journal to take home.
15. Continue until all the groups have completed the activities at this station.

Discussion

1. How close were your hypotheses to the actual results? Explain how you know.
2. Why was the test difficult? What would have made it easier?
3. Which test was the most difficult? Why do you think so?
4. Discuss if any of the other senses would affect the data.
5. Even though you can see them, are there times you need to feel things to find out more information about them? [sometimes you cannot tell if something is warm or cold by looking at it]

Extensions

1. Repeat the activity with gloves but without using the blindfold. Does it make a difference?
2. Repeat the activity with a blindfold, but use different objects (feathers, blocks). How much difference does the shape and weight of the object make?
3. With blindfolds on, give students an object and ask them to identify it.
4. Without allowing students to touch an object, ask them to describe what it feels like (hard, soft, cold, warm, slimy, wet). Why is this hard to do?
5. Try this activity again with cotton balls sprayed with perfume. What additional sense are you now using to find the objects to pick up when you are blindfolded and have gloves on?
6. Use small round jingle bells instead of cotton balls. What additional sense are you now using to find the objects to pick up when you are blindfolded and have gloves on?

Curriculum Correlation

Literature:
   see *Bibliography: Sense of Touch*

Home Link

1. Give students a homework recording sheet made from the class graph blackline and four cotton balls. Have them try the activity on family members and record the numbers picked up by each person tested.
2. Have students try again at home using bottle caps, tissue balls, or other objects of different weight. Are the results different?

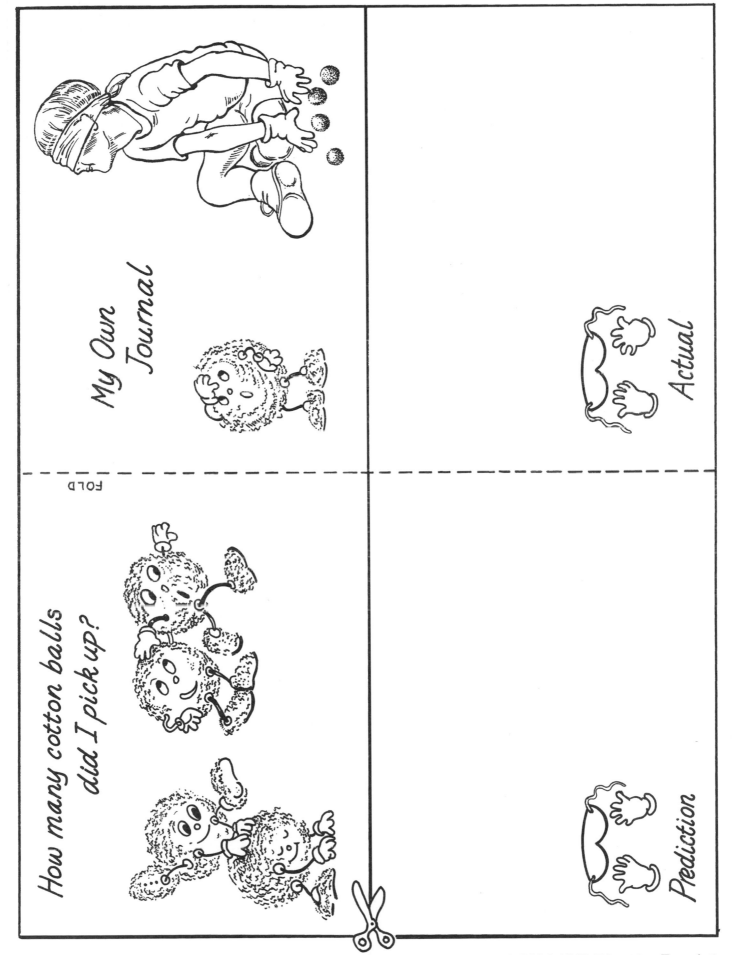

My Own Journal

Actual

How many cotton balls did I pick up?

Prediction

FOLD

Kid Gloves

How many cotton balls can I pick up?

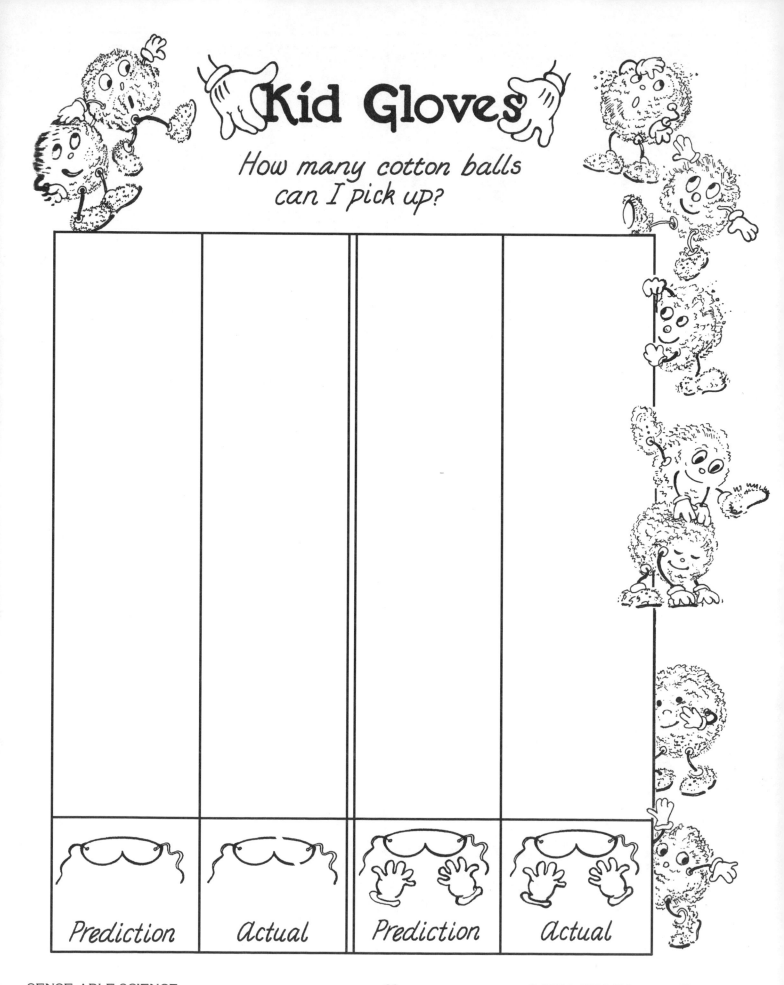

| Prediction | Actual | Prediction | Actual |

Topic
Sense of touch

Key Question
Without using your sense of sight, how can you match a given bead pattern?

Learning Goal
Students will use their sense of touch to complete a given pattern made out of various shaped beads.

Guiding Documents
Project 2061 Benchmarks
- *People use their senses to find out about their surroundings and themselves. Different senses give different information. Sometimes a person can get different information about the same thing by moving closer to it or further away from it.*
- *Describing things as accurately as possible is important in science because it enables people to compare their observations with those of others.*

NCTM Standards 2000*
- *Sort, classify, and order objects by size, number, and other properties*
- *Recognize, describe, and extend patterns such as sequences of sounds and shapes or simple numeric patterns and translate from one representation to another*

Math
Patterning
Tallying

Science
Life science
   human senses

Integrated Processes
Observing
Comparing and contrasting
Predicting
Collecting and recording data
Interpreting data

Materials
Collection of large beads of different shapes
One paper bag per student at the station
String
One tally sheet for each student

Background Information
Exploring, duplicating and creating patterns is an important strategy in problem solving. In science and mathematics we try to find solutions to problems by studying patterns and searching for clues. Student exploration and creation of patterns enables them to better understand and analyze patterns. To begin this exploration and creation of patterns in the primary grades, we begin by looking at patterns made by using an obvious attribute such as shape.

Pattern as it pertains to this activity is defined as *a repeated arrangement of shapes in a linear order*. It is assumed that students will have had multiple experiences in patterning prior to this lesson in which they will be duplicating patterns of beads in a variety of shapes held together on a string. Using only their sense of touch to search for the needed shape, the students will duplicate a given pattern by reaching into a paper bag to find the specific shapes. They will need to search for each shape in the order in which it occurs in the sample pattern.

The students will gain further understanding of the sense of touch in real-world experiences. They will also gain insight into the use of touch by persons who have lost their eyesight.

Management

1. It is suggested that you conduct this lesson at a center or station.
2. Prior to the lesson, string various-shaped beads into repeated patterns. Use approximately eight beads per string. Make enough for one bead pattern per student at the station.
3. Use bead patterns consisting of three of four different shapes: cylindrical, round, square, ovate. Arrange them in patterns such as round, round, square, round, round, square, round, round, square; square, ovate, cylindrical, cylindrical, square, ovate, cylindrical, cylindrical; etc.

4. For each bead pattern, prepare a paper bag containing a string and a duplicate set of the beads you used on the bead patterns.
5. Prepare a tally sheet for each student.

Procedure

1. Show the students the bead patterns you have previously made.
2. Tell them that they will need to make another bead pattern just like the ones in front of them.
3. Tell them that the materials to do this are in the paper sack in front of them, but that they cannot look inside. Ask the *Key Question*.
4. Once the students decide that they can use their sense of touch to distinguish the beads, allow them to begin.
5. Through trial and error, the students will experience how to correctly find the shapes they are looking for to duplicate the patterns.

6. Instruct the students to keep a tally of how many correct and how many incorrect attempts they made to find the correct shapes.

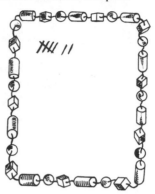

Discussion

1. Why was it difficult to find the shapes you needed? Which shapes were the easiest?...the hardest?
2. Could you use specific colors using only your sense of touch? What sense would you need to use to do this?
3. Would it be more difficult or less difficult to identify the beads using your toes rather than your fingers? Why?

Extensions

1. Allow students to create their own patterns. Have students trade with a partner and try to duplicate each others patterns, using the same touch technique in the paper bag.
2. Allow students to try to duplicate the patterns using their toes to find the needed shapes.

Curriculum Correlation

Literature:
  see *Bibliography: Sense of Touch*

Tally Count

You Tickle My Fancy

Topic
Sense of touch

Key Question
Are your feet or your hands more sensitive to the touch of a feather?

Learning Goal
Students will determine which parts of their body, their feet or their hands, are the most sensitive to the touch of a feather.

Guiding Documents
Project 2061 Benchmarks
- *People use their senses to find out about their surroundings and themselves. Different senses give different information. Sometimes a person can get different information about the same thing by moving closer to it or further away from it*
- *Describing things as accurately as possible is important in science because it enables people to compare their observations with those of others.*

NCTM Standards 2000*
- *Count with understanding and recognize "how many" in sets of objects*
- *Sort and classify objects according to their attributes and organize data about the objects*
- *Represent data using concrete objects, pictures, and graphs*

Math
Number sense
Graphing

Science
Life science
    human senses

Integrated Processes
Observing
Comparing and contrasting
Predicting
Collecting and recording data
Interpreting data

Materials
Feathers
Class graphs
Graph markers

Background Information
    The skin is the major receptor of tactile sensation. We all enjoy the fun and laughter that comes from a good tickle. The tickle is the result of a soft touch to a very sensitive part of our body. This activity uses a feather to determine whether the feet or the hands are more sensitive.

    The sensitivity to touch may vary among humans because of various lifestyles. Those students who have gone barefooted more than others will be less sensitive to the tickle of a feather on their feet than those who rarely go barefooted. The skin on the bottom of the feet of those who go barefoot will callus more than the feet of those who always wear shoes. When the skin is callused, the touch receptors are further from the surface and thus are not as sensitive to touch.

Management
1. Enlarge class graph.
2. Cut out two hand and two foot graph markers for each student.

Procedure
1. Ask the students to remove their shoes and socks. Tell them to find a partner with whom to work.
2. Ask the *Key Question*. Have students show their predictions by placing the appropriate graph markers on the class prediction graph.
3. Direct one student in each pair to gently tickle the palms of the other student's hand, then the sole of the same student's foot.
4. After lots of giggles and jiggles, ask the students who were tickled to record the actual results on the graph of which area was the more ticklish.
5. Have students switch roles and follow the same procedure of tickling and recording actual results.
6. After discussing the results, allow students to test other parts of their bodies: elbows, the tops of their hands, the tops of their feet, the ear lobes, their noses, etc.

Discussion
1. Were all of us the most ticklish on the bottoms of our feet? Why not?
2. Why were some of us more ticklish on the palms of our hands?
3. What sense were we using to feel the tickles?
4. What does our graph tell us about whether our hands or our feet are more sensitive to the touch of a feather?
5. What did you find out about other parts of your body?

*   Reprinted with permission from *Principles and Standards for School Mathematics*, 2000 by the National Council of Teachers of Mathematics. All rights reserved.

Which Is Most Ticklish?

I Think	*I Think*	*I Learned*	*I Learned*

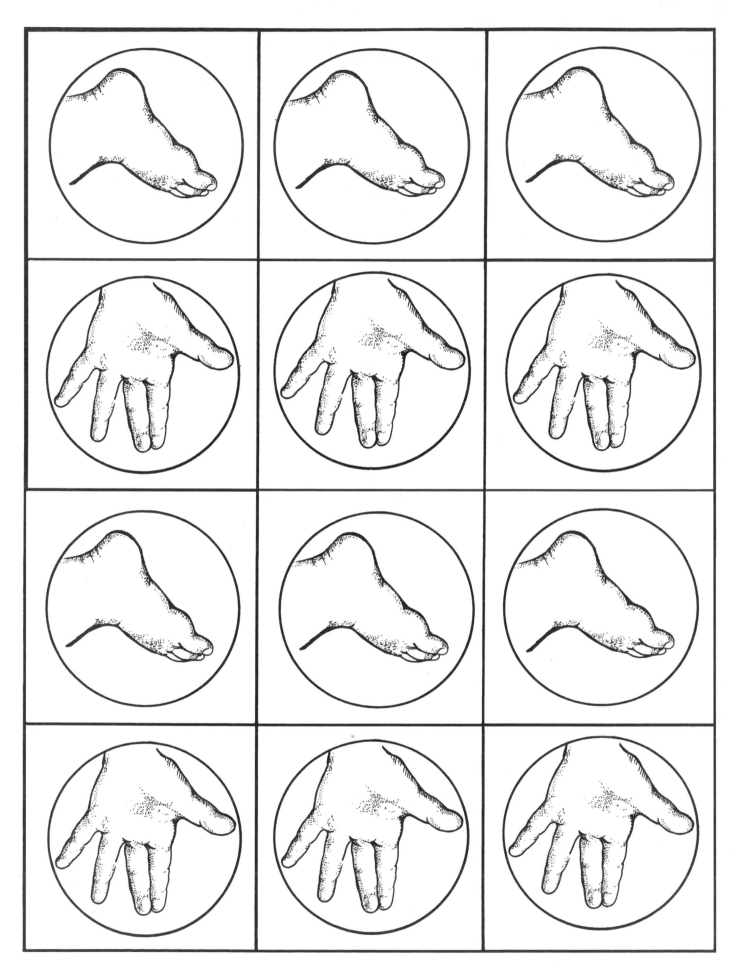

Taste

Amazingly, humans can perceive probably hundreds of distinct tastes, but we only have four taste receptors: sweet, sour, bitter, and salty. Receptors for sweet tastes are located at the tip of the tongue, sour receptors are located on both sides of the tongue, bitter receptors are located at the back of the tongue, and the receptors for salty tastes are located around the edge of the tongue. The variety of tastes we can distinguish is accomplished in two different ways: First a particular substance may stimulate more than one taste receptor, and secondly, our sense of smell strongly affects the tastes we perceive.

Our tongues are covered with receptors, taste buds, which send messages to the brain. Adults may have up to 10,000 taste buds, but babies actually have more. As we get older, the number of taste buds decreases. One problem facing those who care for the elderly is getting them to eat. Their lack of appetite is often due to their inability to detect the flavor of food; therefore, they may lose interest in eating.

It's not uncommon for us to become accustomed to strong tastes. Remember your experiences of tasting some not-so-sweet lemonade on a hot summer day? That first sip really sent your mouth into contortions. After a while, however, you quit puckering and enjoyed your cooling drink.

Taste sensations are sent to the brain relatively slowly compared to smell. The location of the various taste buds also makes a difference.

Have you ever eaten something and experienced a bitter after-taste? Bitter flavors may not be fully sensed until the food passes over the back part of the tongue where the bitter-sensing receptors are located. Sweet flavors register more rapidly because the food touches the receptors on the tip of the tongue as soon as it enters the mouth.

76

Fingernails Are Crunchy

Brenda Dahl

If I could think of all the things
I ate since I was small.
I'd have to have a ream of paper
Just to list them all.

Well, fingernails are crunchy-
But I guess that's not a taste.
I've sampled dirt and crackers
Then let's see . . . there's white school paste.

And surely it makes cookies good-
Though how is hard to tell,
For I've tried vanilla extract
And it's nothing like its smell!

Once I spent the night at grandma's
And 'till now she doubts my word;
That she left it, not the toothpaste,
By my toothbrush . . .seems absurd.

But would I, and all so vividly,
If this had been a dream,
Recall 'till now the awful taste
Of her hair-styling cream?

Another time, out on the porch
My mother came to see,
Since I was sent to feed the pets,
Just what was keeping me.

And there was I, cats all around,
Cats on the porch and underneath,
The can of catfood in my hand,
The spoon between my teeth.

I think it safe for me to say
That sour or salty as the sea,
Of all the tastes there are to taste,
I've tasted a variety.

What Tastes Good To You?

Tune: Turkey In the Straw
Composer: D. Emmett 1859

What tastes good to you?
What are special foods to chew?
Is it chicken that you cook
On the barbecue?
Is it soup you make,
Or some yummy chocolate cake?
What tastes good to you?

What tastes good to you?
Can you give us just a clue?
Is it cocoa that you drink
When the day is through?
Is it ice cream, cool and sweet,
Or the apples that you eat?
What tastes good to you?

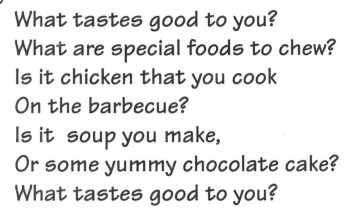

For your tongue can tell,
And it does it very well:
Special taste buds give you taste,
Helped by what you smell.
Salt and sour and sweet
And the bitter things you eat—
Yes, your tongue can tell. . . .

Words by Suzy Gazlay

Seeing Is Not Always Believing

Topic
Sense of taste

Key Question
What senses do we use to tell how substances are different when they all look the same?

Learning Goal
Students will begin to understand that their sense of sight is not always reliable when predicting how something will taste.

Guiding Documents
Project 2061 Benchmarks
- *People use their senses to find out about their surroundings and themselves. Different senses give different information. Sometimes a person can get different information about the same thing by moving closer to it or further away from it*
- *Describing things as accurately as possible is important in science because it enables people to compare their observations with those of others.*

NCTM Standards 2000*
- *Count with understanding and recognize "how many" in sets of objects*
- *Sort and classify objects according to their attributes and organize data about the objects*
- *Represent data using concrete objects, pictures, and graphs*

Math
Charting
Logical thinking

Science
Life science
    human senses

Integrated Processes
Observing
Comparing and contrasting
Predicting
Classifying
Applying

Materials
For the class:
    4 clear sipper-type plastic bags
    1/2 cup salt
    1/2 cup flour
    1/2 cups powdered sugar
    1/2 cup granulated sugar
    water
    butcher paper (see *Management 5*)
    Venn diagram(see *Management 6*)

For each student:
    hand lens
    plastic spoon
    paper plate (see *Management 3*)
    Student Recording Sections
    3-oz. paper cup
    scissors
    glue
    crayons

Background Information
The taste buds on our tongues contain sensory receptors which provide us with information about whether something is sweet, salty, bitter, sour, or combinations of the four. The sense of sight helps us to anticipate the taste of foods. When the substances look very similar, it is often a surprise to find that they actually taste different. This activity has students trying to identify the tastes of substances which are very similar in appearance.

Management
1. This activity is best done in small group settings. Learning stations are highly recommended.

2. An adult supervisor is essential in ensuring that this activity is successful.

3. Prior to the activity, use a marker to divide paper plates into 4 sections Number the sections 1-4.

4. Copy *Student Recording Sections*-one page per student.

5. Prepare a class chart by dividing butcher paper into four sections. This should be large enough to accommodate the sections from cut quarters

Things that remind me of...	
Salt	
Powdered Sugar	
Sugar	
Flour	

6. Enlarge the two-circle Venn diagram with the labels: sweet, salty.

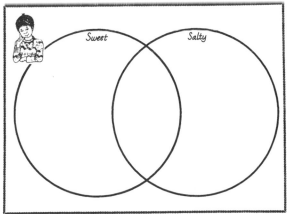

7. Number the four plastic bags. Put 1/2 cup salt into bag #1, 1/2 cup powdered sugar into bag #2, 1/2 cup flour into bag #3, and 1/2 cup of sugar into bag #4.

Procedures

1. Allow the students to look at the four plastic bag containing samples of each of the substances you have prepared for them to taste. Ask them if they can tell just by looking at the substances as to what each one is. Allow the students to give suggestions as to what each substance may or may not be. 2. Make a temporary class graph on the chalk board to record their predictions as to what each bag may contain.

3. Ask the *Key Question* and discuss the dangers of tasting unknown substances without adult supervision. Reassure students that these substances are not poisonous.

4. Distribute the *Student Recording Sections* activity sheet. Have the students number the sections.

5. Give students plastic spoons, the quartered paper plates, and a small cup of water. Direct them to put approximately 1/4-1/2 teaspoon of the first substance (salt) onto their plate making certain that substance #1 goes onto section #1 of their paper plate.

6. Before the students taste the first substance, give each student a hand lens to look closely at the substance. Discuss what it looks like (the crystal shape), what it smells like, etc.

7. Ask the students if they want to change their original prediction of what they think the substance might be. Let them taste the substance.

8. Have the students taste each of the four substances following the same procedure. Be sure to let them take a small sip of water between each taste to clean their palates. Ask what they think each substance was. If they do not fknow, tell them the actual substance.

9. If any substances are left on the plates, have students shake them off into the trash can. Direct students to draw foods that have the taste of the mystery substance in the appropriate section of the paper plate. (Examples:chips, candy, pancakes, frosting) You may want to label the drawings.

10. Have students cut their paper plates into the four sections and glue them onto the chart (see *Figure 1, Management*).

11. Using the *Student Recording Sections* activity page, ask the students to draw something (or paste in pictures from old magazines) in the numbered sections. Section #1 should have a picture of something salty; #2, something made with powdered sugar; #3, something made with flour; and #4, something made with sugar. Have the students cut these sections out and use on a class Venn diagram (see *Figure 2, Management*).

Discussion

1. When we looked at these substances and noticed that they looked a lot alike, what sense did we decide to use to tell if they were the same or different?
2. Let's look at each of the numbered sections on our class chart and see what we thought each of the substances tasted like. (Go through each of the chart sections.)
3. What did you use to find out what these things tasted like? [tongue]
4. What part of our body contains the sense of taste? [mouth, tongue]
5. How does your tongue help you taste? (Discuss taste buds)
6. Where are your taste buds located? (If you have a mirror you may want students to observe the taste buds on their tongues.)
7. Why should we not taste things when there are no adults around to supervise?
8. Do some foods taste both sweet and salty? Let's look at our Venn diagram and see which ones taste just sweet…just salty…both? Do we all agree about the tastes? Why not?
9. Everyone is different, we taste things differently. Some of us like foods that others don't. Humans are different in many ways.

Extensions

1. Read *A Tasting Party* by Jane Belk Moncure (Children's Press, Chicago, 1982). Have the students organize a tasting party of their own. Use one suggested in the book or see if students can come up with something different.
2. Do the same activity with liquids: ≠water; flat, clear soda; clear gelatin dissolved in water, white vinegar, sugar water.
3. Do the same activity with peeled fruits and vegetables: apples, potatoes, pears.
4. Using wrappers from the students' lunches (or pictures of food items) graph them according to the attributes of salty, sweet, and sour.

Curriculum Correlation

Language Arts:
  See *Appendix. Bibliography: Sense of Taste*

Home Links

1. Ask students to find things that are salty or sweet at home. Draw pictures to represent these items.
2. Ask students to keep a record of the number of foods that are salty or sweet that they ate for breakfast, or lunch, or dinner.

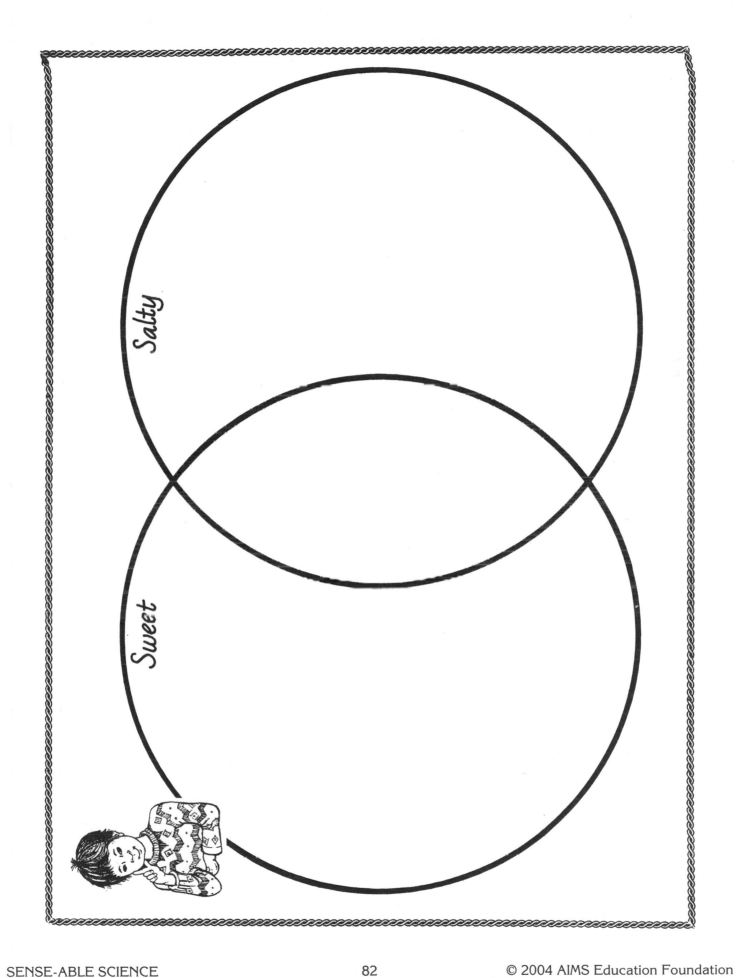

Salty

Sweet

82

Student recording sections.

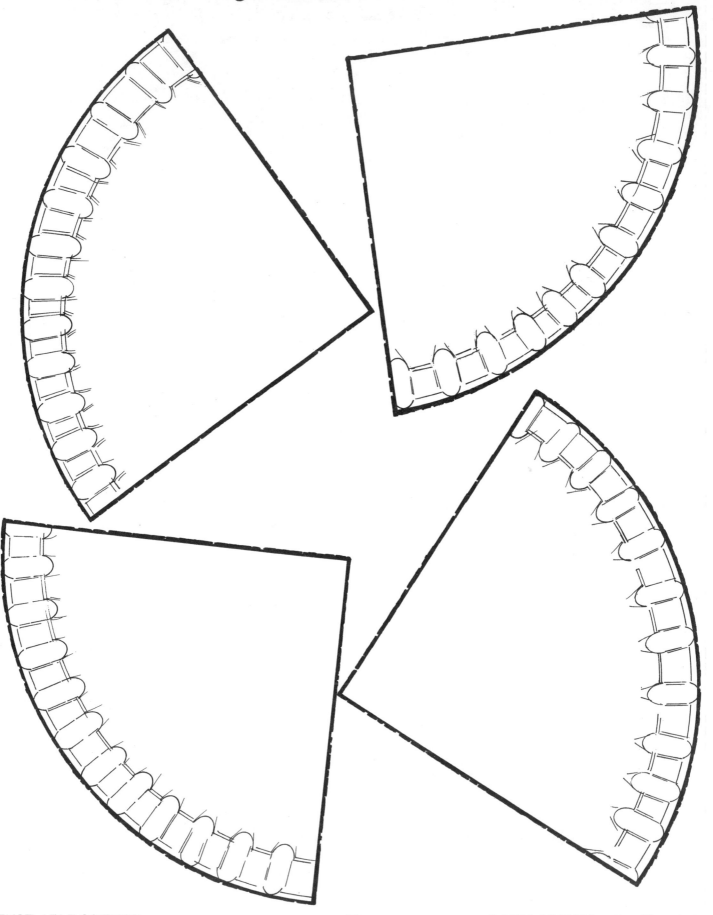

83

EGGS-TRA SPECIAL SCRAMBLE

Topic
Sense of taste

Key Question
How will the color of the eggs affect how they taste?

Learning Goal
Students will become aware of how the sense of taste is affected by the sense of sight.

Guiding Documents
Project 2061 Benchmarks
- *People use their senses to find out about their surroundings and themselves. Different senses give different information. Sometimes a person can get different information about the same thing by moving closer to it or further away from it*
- *Describing things as accurately as possible is important in science because it enables people to compare their observations with those of others.*

NCTM Standards 2000*
- *Count with understanding and recognize "how many" in sets of objects*
- *Sort and classify objects according to their attributes and organize data about the objects*
- *Represent data using concrete objects, pictures, and graphs*

Math
Graphing
Number sense and numeration

Science
Life science
   human senses

Integrated Processes
Observing
Comparing and contrasting
Collecting and recording data
Interpreting data
Predicting

Materials
For the class:
   Green Eggs and Ham by Dr. Seuss
   2 class graphs
   glue sticks
   1-2 dozen eggs (depending on class size)
   1 or 2 electric skillets or hot plate and skillets
   butter or non-stick cooking spray
   green food coloring
   milk
   salt and pepper
   spatula

For each student:
   graph markers (see *Management 1*)
   paper plate
   fork

Background Information
Your tongue sends messages to the brain about what you eat. The tongue is covered with tastebuds. There are four different types of taste buds: for sweet, sour, bitter, and salty things. Your tongue is not the only important sense in tasting. The senses of smell and sight also play important roles. If you closed your eyes and held your nose, you may not be able to tell the difference between an apple and a potato. The message your sense of sight sends the brain before you even taste the food, often plays an important role in determining likes and dislikes.

Management

1. Prepare two class graphs by enlarging them with an opaque projector or with an overhead projector. One will be used for predictions and one for actual results.
2. Cut out the graph markers; each student will need two markers.
3. Set up cooking area. Another adult could cook one batch of eggs if two skillets are available or simply do the cooking procedure twice.

Procedure

1. Read the book *Green Eggs and Ham* by Dr. Seuss.
2. Ask how many students have eaten green eggs? How do you think they would taste? Would they taste the same as yellow eggs?
3. Ask how we could determine if they taste the same?
4. Show students one graph and explain that they will use it to record their predictions about how they think the eggs will taste.
5. Distribute graph markers. Instruct students to write their names on one of their markers. Have them glue their marker in the appropriate section of the prediction graph.
6. Make two sets of scrambled eggs, one green and one yellow, by beating eggs, milk, salt and pepper in two bowls. Add green food coloring to one of the egg mixtures and cook in buttered or sprayed, non-stick pans.
7. Give each student a small portion of each type of egg on the paper plate.
8. Taste the green eggs and discuss how they taste.
9. Taste the yellow eggs. Discuss.
10. Distribute the second set of graph markers for recording on the second graph representing the actual taste. Let students glue their markers in the section they choose.
11. Compare the two graphs.

Discussion

1. How are the two graphs different?
2. How close were your predictions to the final results?
3. Does anybody know what was added to change the color? Does food coloring have a flavor? If it does not have a flavor could it change the flavor of food?
4. How did our eyes change how we felt about the food? How did our eyes change the taste of the food?

Extensions

1. Taste white and dark chocolate. Discuss their similarities and differences.
2. Reread the book, *Green Eggs and Ham,* and discuss how the animal in the book changed his mind about green eggs. What made him change his mind?
3. Discuss or show other foods that are different colors than expected such as red pears or broccoflower.

Curriculum Correlation

Literature:
   see *Bibliography: Sense of Taste*

Language Arts:
   Using the framework in the Dr. Seuss book, write a poem about a funny-colored food. Let students draw pictures of foods that are different colors and share their work.

Home Link

   Send home the recipe for eggs and ask if anyone wants to try other colors of eggs and report to the class on it.

*   Reprinted with permission from *Principles and Standards for School Mathematics*, 2000 by the National Council of Teachers of Mathematics. All rights reserved.

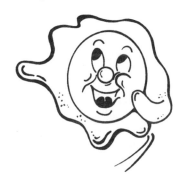

Do green and yellow eggs taste the same?

Same   **Different**

EGGS-TRA SPECIAL SCRAMBLE

Color and cut out eggs for use as graph markers.

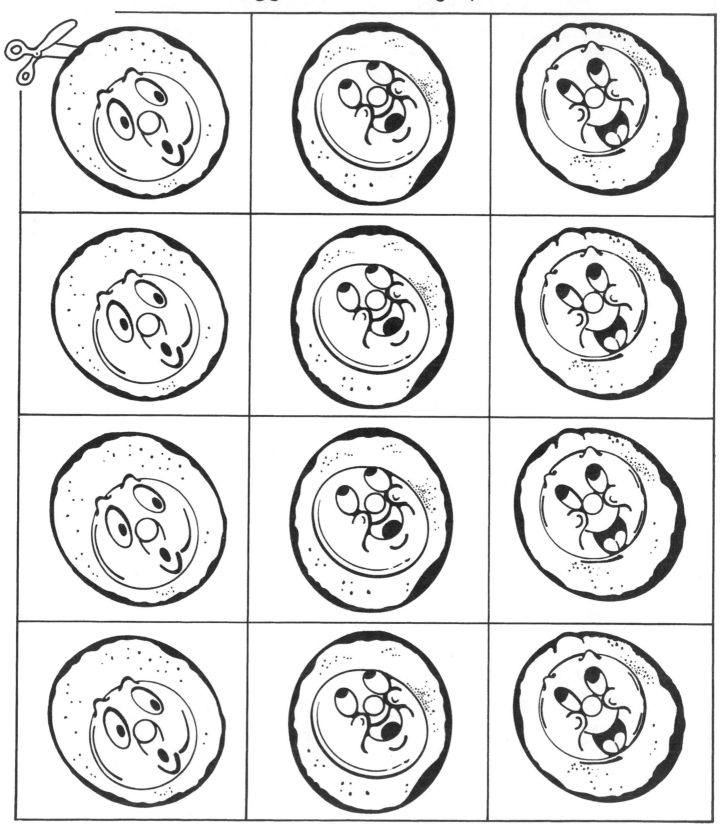

Make Mine Porridge

Topic
Sense of taste

Key Question
How do you decide if you like one kind of food better than another?

Learning Goal
Students will compare the taste of three kinds of porridge.

Guiding Documents
Project 2061 Benchmarks
- *People use their senses to find out about their surroundings and themselves. Different senses give different information. Sometimes a person can get different information about the same thing by moving closer to it or further away from it*
- *Describing things as accurately as possible is important in science because it enables people to compare their observations with those of others.*

NCTM Standards 2000*
- *Count with understanding and recognize "how many" in sets of objects*
- *Sort and classify objects according to their attributes and organize data about the objects*
- *Represent data using concrete objects, pictures, and graphs*

Math
Graphing
Number sense and numeration
Measuring
Logical reasoning

Science
Life science
    human senses

Integrated Processes
Observing
Comparing and contrasting
Collecting and recording data

Interpreting data
Inferring

Materials
For the class:
    Goldilocks and the Three Bears
    cornmeal
    Cream of Wheat
    salt, optional
    margarine, optional
    water
    hot plate or microwave
    cooking pot or bowl
    wooden spoon
    measuring spoons
    measuring cups
    Yum and Yuk chart, enlarged
    Yum and Yuk Venn diagram
    My Favorite Porridge graph

For each student:
    1 plastic spoon
    1 small paper plate
    1 set of graphing markers
    1 student book

Background Information
Students need many opportunities to explore food and cooking. In this activity, students will explore the taste and texture of food. They will focus on the "cooked" texture as they taste and compare three kinds of cereal and choose their favorite and least liked. They will observe the changes brought about by the addition of water and heat to the dry cereals.

Management
1. Prior to class, enlarge the class graph, the *Yum and Yuk* chart, and the Venn diagram. You may choose to use one, two, or all three representations of data; the variety is provided for your convenience, or use the AIMS large graph chart and Venn diagram.
2. Use the recipe guides on the boxes of cereal for

preparation. Prepare a quantity according to the number of students in your class. Each student will probably need about one-fourth of a normal serving.

3. This activity can be done in a variety of ways depending on your adult-to-student ratio.
   * divide the class into groups, each preparing one of the cereals and coming together to taste, compare, and discuss the textures
   * teacher demonstrates the preparation of the cereals to the class involving the students as helpers, then they proceed with comparing taste and texture
   * reduce the recipe into individual portions and allow each student to make his or her own cereal. **Caution: You will be using very hot water in the preparation of these cereals.**

4. A set of graphing markers is necessary if you are using all three representations of data. A set of markers consists of:
   * three *Yum* and three *Yuk* markers for the *Yum and Yuk Chart* (Because you do not know student responses, you will need to make extra markers.)
   * two graphing markers with students' names: one for the Venn diagram and another for the *My Favorite Porridge* graph.

Procedure

1. Ask students if they have heard the story of *Goldilocks and the Three Bears*. Ask them to briefly recall the storyline. You may want to read one or several versions of the story at this time.
2. Direct the students to think about which senses the characters are using in the story.
3. Discuss what porridge is and what kind the bears may have left to cool.
4. Ask the students how they could find out whether they like porridge or not. [taste some]
5. Have students observe and describe the cereal before it is prepared.
6. Prepare the cereals by following package directions. Let students help by allowing them to do any of the following: measure, pour, and stir (before temperature gets to the boiling stage). **Caution: Hot cereals bubble when boiling. Have students maintain a safe distance from boiling cereal.**
7. Let the cereals cool.
8. Place a teaspoonful of one of the cereals on the students' tasting plates.
9. Discuss how the cereal looks after it has been cooked.
10. Tell students the name of the cereal and have them taste it.
11. Have students color and cut appropriate *Yum /Yuk Markers* and place them on the *Yum and Yuk Chart.*
12. Follow the same procedure for the other two cereals.
13. Have students cut out and write their names on two graphing markers. Direct them to place their markers in the appropriate column on the *My Favorite Porridge* graph and in the appropriate area of the Venn diagram.

Discussion

1. How did the cereal change after it was cooked? Does there seem to be more cereal after it is cooked? Why do you think this happens?
2. Will cooking all kinds of cereal do the same thing that happened to these cereals? Explain your answer.
3. What do you think would happen if we cooked the cold cereal some of you eat in the morning?
4. What made our cereal change? [water and heat]
5. If we were going to do this again, what cereal might we use?
6. Compare the class results from the chart, graph, and Venn diagram.
7. Is one cereal better than another because more students like it? Explain.
8. By looking at the results on our chart and graph, if we were going to make a breakfast for this class, would we need to make all three cereals? Explain.

Extensions

1. Talk about the other senses used by the story characters in various scenes.
2. Have each student make a copy of the class graph by coloring pictures in each column to represent the number of likes and dislikes for each of the three cereals.

Curriculum Correlation

Literature:
1. Marshall, Jones. *Goldilocks and the Three Bears.* Dial Books, New York. 1988.
2. Turkle, Brinton. *Deep in the Forest.* Dutton Children Books, New York. 1976.
3. see *Bibliography: Sense of Taste*

Language Arts:
1. Write recipes for making your favorite cereal.
2. Teach the students the poem *Make Mine Porridge.*

Home Links

1. Have a taste test with the family.
2. Graph the results of your family's most and least favorite cereals.
3. Help cook your favorite cereal at home for the family.
4. Watch a parent cook your favorite cereal to see if he/she follows the same steps.
5. Bring in your favorite cereal for a tasting party.
6. Make a list of food you could cook for breakfast.

* Reprinted with permission from *Principles and Standards for School Mathematics*, 2000 by the National Council of Teachers of Mathematics. All rights reserved.

Yum and Yuk Chart

| Yum | Yuk | Yum | Yuk | Yum | Yuk |

Color and cut out markers for Yum and Yuk chart.

yum-m-m   yum-m-m   yum-m-m

yuk-k-k   yuk-k-k   yuk-k-k

yum-m-m   yum-m-m   yum-m-m

yuk-k-k   yuk-k-k   yuk-k-k

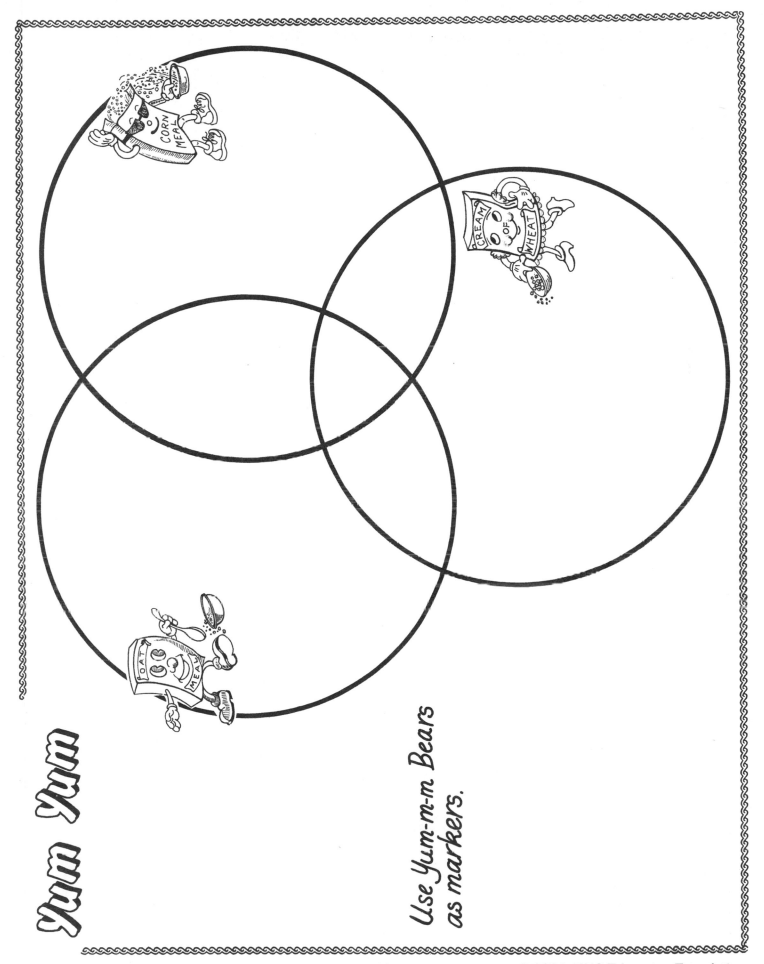

Yum Yum

Use Yum-m-m Bears as markers.

My Favorite Porridge

Color and cut out markers for My Favorite Porridge Graph and the Yum-Yum Venn Diagram. Write your name on the bowl.

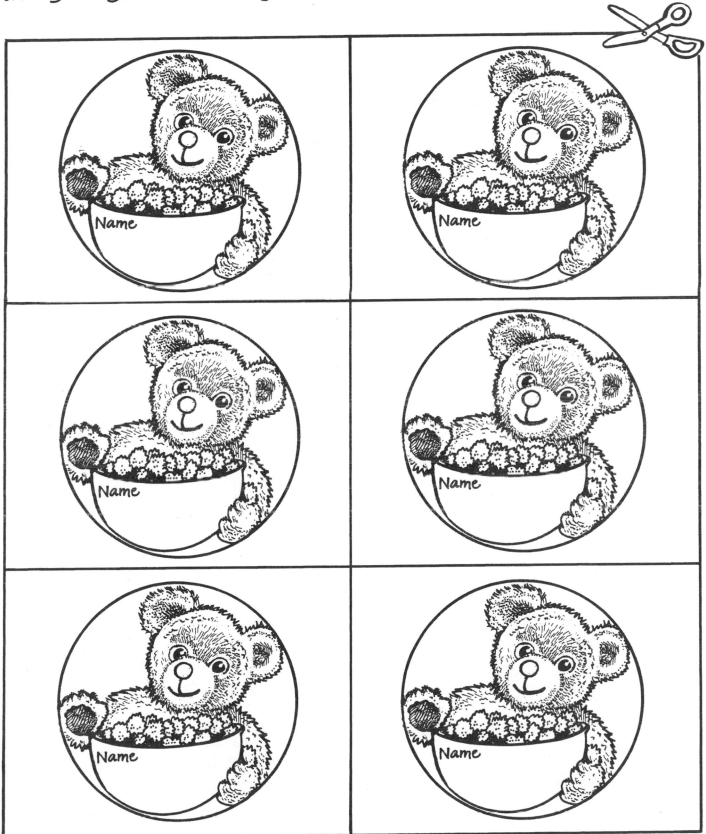

Make Mine Porridge

Three bears: small, medium, and large,
Are planning for a feast,
So they must choose their favorite dish,
And which they like the least.

They start the list with porridges:
Creamed wheat, cornmeal, and oat.
They sample each, then once again—
And now it's time to vote.

Brenda Dahl

Margo
Pocock

THE ART OF TASTING

Topic
Senses of smell and taste

Key Question
What do you think we use when we taste something?

Learning Goal
Student will discover that they use their taste buds and noses to help them taste foods.

Guiding Document
Project 2061 Benchmarks
- *People use their senses to find out about their surroundings and themselves. Different senses give different information. Sometimes a person can get different information about the same thing by moving closer to it or further away from it*
- *Describing things as accurately as possible is important in science because it enables people to compare their observations with those of others.*

Math
Tallying
Number sense and numeration

Science
Life science
    human senses

Integrated Processes
Observing
Comparing and contrasting
Communicating
Applying

Materials
For the class:
    chart paper
    markers
    12 x 18-inch construction paper
    legal-sized envelopes

For each student:
    a variety of foods that represent salty, sour, and
        sweet tastes (see *Management 1*)
    student response cards (see *Management 4*)
    pocket response holder mat (see *Management 5*)

Background Information
Your sense of smell and taste work in conjunction with each other. Even the slightest odor can influence the way most foods taste to you. When you have a cold and your nasal passages are plugged, you may experience a loss of taste, or taste discrimination.

Management
1. Collect different foods which represent the salty, sour, and sweet tastes. Some examples would be corn chips or potato chips, lemons, green apples, butterscotch candy.
2. Prepare bite-sized portions of these items.
3. Prepare chart (see *Figure 1*).
4. Duplicate student response cards on card stock. Cut out one set per student for each food they will be tasting. You may wish to color and laminate these response cards to enable you to use them in future activities. It is suggested that you color code the "yes" cards a different color than the "no" cards so they will be easily distinguishable during the activity.
5. Prepare one pocket response holder mat for each student. Duplicate one each of the following pocket labels for each mat:
   - "yes" (holding nose)
   - "no" (holding nose)
   - "yes" (not holding nose)
   - "no" (not holding nose)
   Cut and glue these labels on pockets made from legal-size envelopes which have been sealed and

cut in half vertically. Glue or tape these pockets to a 12" x 18" piece of construction paper.

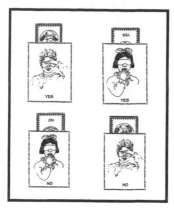

Figure 1

Procedure

1. Have students wear their blindfolds and hold their noses while you place a peppermint candy into each of their mouths. Tell them to be sure to hold their noses closed with their fingers until you tell them otherwise.

2. When all students have a peppermint, ask them if they can identify the flavor of the candy while continuing to hold their noses. Quickly record student responses on the chart paper.

3. Ask the students if they can taste the object in their mouth. Instruct them to push their blindfolds up on their foreheads so they can see, but continue to hold their noses closed. Have them put their response card in the appropriate pocket on their response holder mats. ("Yes" or "no" holding nose)

4. Direct all the students to let go of their noses. Ask them if they can now determine the flavor of the candy. Record their responses on the chart.

5. Tell the students to place a response card in the appropriate pocket to tell you if they can or cannot taste the candy. ("Yes" or "no" not holding nose)

6. Repeat *Procedures 1- 4* using different foods (see *Management 1*).

Discussion

1. Were you able to tell the flavor of the food you were eating while holding your nose?

2. Which of the foods that you tasted did you need to be able to smell before you could tell what they were?

3. Look in your response pockets, how many of you had to smell the food before you could taste it? How do you know this?

4. Which food (sour, sweet, or salty) was easiest to taste without smelling it?...hardest?

5. Sometimes, when you have a bad cold, can you taste your food? Can you smell things when you have a bad cold? Why do you think this happens?

Extensions

1. Bring in other foods and continue the taste test.

2. Graph the class results using the response cards.

Curriculum Correlation

Literature:

see *Bibliography: Sense of Taste, Sense of Smell*

NO

NO

YES

YES

Student Response Cards

NO

YES

Student Response Labels

YES

NO

YES

NO

TASTE BUD MAPPING

Topic
Sense of taste

Key Question
Where on our tongue do we taste sweet, sour, and salty flavors?

Learning Goal
Students will discover that different areas on the tongue are more sensitive to sweet, salty, and sour tastes.

Guiding Document
Project 2061 Benchmarks
- *People use their senses to find out about their surroundings and themselves. Different senses give different information. Sometimes a person can get different information about the same thing by moving closer to it or further away from it*
- *Describing things as accurately as possible is important in science because it enables people to compare their observations with those of others.*

Science
Life science
  human senses

Integrated Processes
Observing
Comparing and contrasting
Predicting
Collecting and recording data
Interpreting data
Applying

Materials
For the class:
  3 cups of lemon juice
  3 cups of sugar water
  3 cups of salt water

For each student:
  6 cotton swabs
  12 x 18-inch piece of white construction paper
  clown labels (see *Management 4*)

pencil or crayon
cup of water
small mirror

Background Information
Although we perceive probably hundreds of distinct tastes, there are only four types of taste receptors: sweet, sour, salty, and bitter. The variety of tastes is produced in two ways. First, a particular substance may stimulate two or more receptor types to different degrees (for example, salty sour). More importantly, material being tasted usually gives off molecules into the air inside the mouth. These molecules diffuse to the olfactory receptors. Our sense of smell seems to enhance the taste of the food. The relationship between our senses of smell and taste is evident when our sense of smell is diminished in some way. Most of us have experienced the "tastelessness" of normally savory foods when we have colds in which our nasal passages are plugged.

Management
1. You will need adult helpers with this activity. They will be using cotton swabs to drop small amounts of liquids on the students' tongues in specific areas.
2. Prepare the liquids in the following manner:
   - sour - 100% lemon juice can be purchased in grocery stores
   - salty - dissolve 3 tablespoons of salt in 3 cups of water
   - sweet - dissolve 3 tablespoons of sugar in 3 cups of water
3. Because of the nature of the taste of bitter, and because of the location of the bitter taste receptors, we do not suggest including a bitter taste test in this activity. The bitter taste receptors are located at the back of the tongue. The application of a bitter liquid with a cotton swab may cause some

children to gag or choke. For these reasons, we will not be including bitter in this activity.

4. Students will draw a large tongue on the construction paper. Copy two sets (one page) of clown labels for each student to be used to indicate whether or not students could distinguish sour, salty, and sweet tastes on various parts of their tongues.

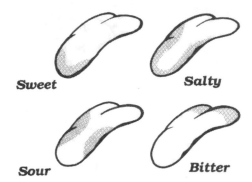

Sweet

Salty

Sour

Bitter

Procedure

1. Encourage students to use a mirror to look closely at the surface of their tongues. Point out the small raised bumps on their tongues and tell them that these are called taste buds.
2. Inform students that some taste buds are for tasting things that are sour, some are for tasting things that are salty, and some are for tasting things that are sweet.
3. Tell them that they will be drawing a map of the areas of the tongue where they can taste those three things: salty, sour, and sweet.
4. Have them draw a large picture of a tongue on the construction paper. Encourage them to use most of the paper for their drawing. This drawing will be their *Taste Bud Map.*
5. Inform them that an adult will be dropping a small amount of salt water, sugar water, and lemon juice on different parts of their tongue.
6. Allow the students to look into a mirror as the adult drops the liquid on their tongues so that they can see where the liquid is being placed.
7. Start with the lemon juice. Soak a cotton swab in the lemon juice. Apply this cotton swab to the side of the tongue. Direct the students to glue the appropriate clown face on the *Taste Bud Map* in the area tested. The smiling clown represents that they could taste the lemon juice, the frowning clown represents that they could not taste it.
8. Allow the students to sip some water to clear their palates.
9. Using a new cotton swab, apply the lemon juice to the tip of the tongue. Students should now record whether or not they could taste the sour lemon juice at this location. Again instruct the students sip some water.
10. Continue this procedure with the sugar water and

the salt water. Use a new cotton swab for each test. Allow the students to take a sip of water between each test. Be sure to first test the liquids in the area where the specific taste receptors are located and then in another area where they are not supposed to be able to taste it. Record each time.

11. Direct the students to color the correct clown face in their student journals.

Discussion

1. Did you taste the sour lemon juice when you put it on the tip of your tongue? How do you know?
2. Could you taste salty at all the different places? How about in the middle of your tongue?
3. Sometimes things taste salty and sweet. Why do you think this happens? [your taste buds work together, the food gets on both of them so you taste both]
4. If you had a cold, do you think you could taste these flavors? Why or why not?

Extension

Use solid foods instead of the cotton swabs and liquids.

Curriculum Correlation

Literature:
   see *Bibliography*: *Sense of Taste*

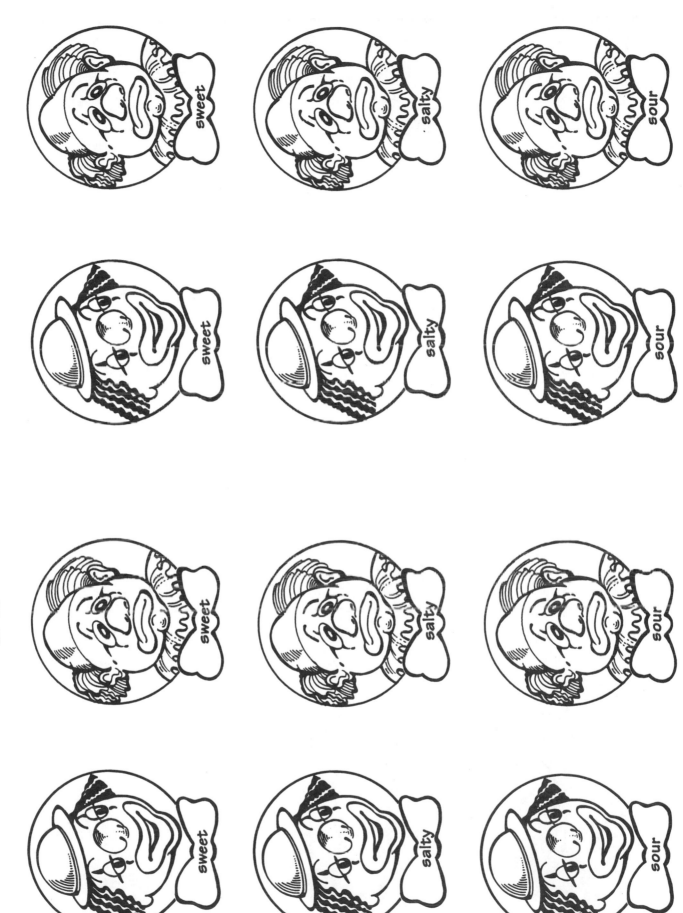

Taste Bud Mapping Markers

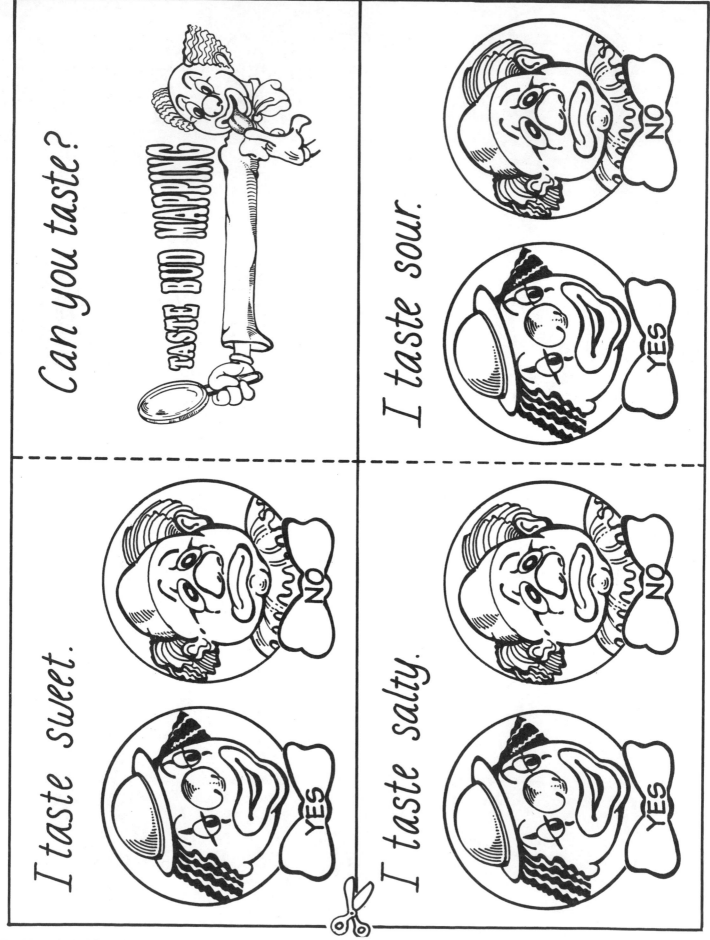

Can you taste?

TASTE BUD MAPPING

I taste sour.   NO   YES

I taste sweet.   NO   YES

I taste salty.   NO   YES

Smell

What smells better than to walk into your house and smell freshly baked bread? Maybe it's the smell of a clean baby or your favorite cologne or the outdoor smell at a summer cabin. Smells are powerful forces for triggering memories.

The sense of smell, or olfaction, originates in your nose. When you inhale, you can feel the air being drawn into your nose. This air is filled with odor molecules which flow through your nasal cavity where they encounter hair-like projections that are covered with a layer of mucus. The mucus dissolves the odor molecules so they can be sampled by the receptors. Because you are always breathing, you are always monitoring the odors in the air. When you want to smell something in more detail, all you have to do is take a good sniff to bring more air into your nasal cavity. This causes more odor molecules to pass over the olfactory hairs helping you to better perceive the smell.

Sometimes the sense of smell gets desensitized. If you walk into a room where a scented candle has been burning, you might notice the odor at once. Yet, after a while, you no longer notice it. The sense of smell responds mainly to changes in stimuli. Once you become accustomed, or desensitized, to the smell, it may have to increase up to 300 times in strength before you notice it again. This helps prevent you from becoming overloaded with unimportant information and is a good example of how your brain acts as a filter of information. The people who live in the house may be so used to the smell of the scented candle that they do not notice it. However, if they have a natural gas leak, they would notice this odor even though they were not conscious of the scent of the candle. The natural gas leak represents a change in the smells to which they were accustomed.

The sense of taste and the sense of smell are very closely linked. When you eat food, it gives off odor molecules that travel up the connecting passage between your mouth and your nose. The odor molecules enter the nasal cavity stimulating the smell receptors. The food's flavor is a result not only of what is tasted but also what is smelled. You've surely noticed that when you have a cold, your food doesn't seem to have as much flavor. This is because your nose is blocked by thick mucus that doesn't allow the odor molecules to penetrate.

Compared to other animals, you do not have an especially good sense of smell. Dogs are often trained to track people or sniff out certain substances such as drugs. They are able to do this because they may have 100 million olfactory receptors compared to your five million!

Especially for You

Brenda Dahl

My mom is not at home today.
The rain outside is splashing down,
And though I can't go out to play,
I love the earth smells all around.

My grandma's come to stay with me.
My grandpa's here as well.
My house is filled up pleasingly
With every wondrous smell.

There's onion, roast and garlic,
Warm yeasty breads of wheat and rye,
Ginger, cloves, burned candlewick,
And wet galoshes left to dry.

A thunder clap! And like a flash,
Throwing wide the kitchen door,
In slides my Irish Setter, Splash,
'Cross grandma's new-waxed kitchen floor.

My grandma isn't smiling — yet.
Her nose is wrinkled up.
"Oh, Splash! You smell just horrid wet!"
She scolds my dripping pup.

Yet 'mid all this confusion, a warm familiar smell,
Drifts in among the others, and simply lingers there.
I turn, and in the doorway, I'd heard no knock or bell,
My Mom and Dad just watch and smile, while I just stand and stare.

My mom kneels down upon the rug, so I sit down there too.
She says, "I've brought home something, just especially for you."
The something that she hands me is all wriggly, wrapped in blue.
It's the tiniest baby sister - when I kiss her -
She smells—New!

My Sense of Smell

Tune: Animal Fair

I have a sense of smell
And it helps me to tell
When food tastes good
They way it should
It does its job quite well.
I smell a summer breeze
Sometimes it makes me sneeze.
My nose can tell
The wonderful smell
Of flowers, grass, and trees.

Now what can that smell be?
I smell but I can't see
My mom's perfume
Across the room
It sure smells good to me!
I love to smell the sea,
A piney Christmas tree,
I'd love to tell
My favorite smell
Won't you tell yours to me?

Words by Suzy Gazlay

Topic
Sense of smell

Key Questions
1. Do you think you can identify what an object is by just smelling it?
2. What do some smells remind you of?

Learning Goal
Student will become aware of the information given to them through the sense of smell.

Guiding Documents
Project 2061 Benchmarks
- *People use their senses to find out about their surroundings and themselves. Different senses give different information. Sometimes a person can get different information about the same thing by moving closer to it or further away from it*
- *Describing things as accurately as possible is important in science because it enables people to compare their observations with those of others.*

NCTM Standards 2000*
- *Count with understanding and recognize "how many" in sets of objects*
- *Sort and classify objects according to their attributes and organize data about the objects*
- *Represent data using concrete objects, pictures, and graphs*

Math
Charting
Graphing

Science
Life science
    human senses

Integrated Processes
Observing
Classifying
Predicting
Comparing and contrasting
Collecting and recording data
Interpreting data

Materials
For the class:
    Our Smell Chart (see *Management 4*)

For a station:
    4 empty 35 mm film canisters with lids

diced onion pieces
orange sections
3 tablespoons ground coffee
bar of soap cut into small pieces
scissors
tape
crayons

For each child:
    student recording sheet
    clipboard (see *Appendix: Science Tools*)
    crayons and/or pencils
    My Home Smells Nice student booklet (see *Management 5*)

Background Information
There are about 5 million olfactory receptors in the human nose. These receptors give humans the ability to discriminate approximately 10,000 different odors. Even though this seems like an extraordinary feat, our olfactory abilities compare very poorly to those of other mammals. The sense of smell guides animal behavior more than any other sense. Dogs use their noses to explore things around them in the same way we humans use our eyes. A dog's olfactory sense is many, many times more sensitive than ours. Despite this great difference, humans find smells to be distinctive, identifiable, and memorable.

Management
1. Poke a few small holes in the top of each film canister lid.

2. Place the onion in one film canister, the orange into another, coffee into a third, and the soap bits into the last. Number the film canisters using a permanent marker.
3. At each station you will need to provide the following: the four filled and numbered film canisters, student recording sheets, crayons, and scissors.
4. Enlarge the *Our Smell Chart* to record the students' predictions.
5. Prepare a *My Home Smells Nice* booklet for each child. Cut apart and staple on the left side.
6. This activity is best taught in two parts. The first

part involves students in small groups determining and charting the mystery contents of film canisters. The second part asks students to relate scents to different memories—walking or riding to school, home scents, etc.

Procedure
Part One:

1. Hand out the student recording sheets with the pictures of numbered film canisters.Have students attach sheets to their clipboards to provide a smooth writing surface.
2. Show students how to fan the air above the canister toward their noses in order to smell the contents. After allowing the students to smell each canister, have them draw their predictions of the contents in the appropriately numbered canister on the recording sheet.

3. When the group is finished smelling the canisters, the students will cut on the broken lines of their papers and place the numbered drawings in the appropriate columns on the enlarged *Our Smell Chart.*
4. Invite other groups to the station until all class members have made their predictions and contributed to the chart.
5. Share the finished chart with the entire class.

Discussion
Part One:

1. What did your nose tell you about canister number one?
2. Are the objects pictured in column one of our chart the same? What does this tell us? (Use this technique for all four columns.)
3. What can we say about these four containers?
4. What does your nose tell you about what was in the containers that your eyes did not?
5. When you smelled the contents of the containers, did it make you think of home or a special time or place? Explain.

Procedure
Part Two:

1. Fold a piece of 8 1/2 X 11-inch paper in fourths. Number the sections of the paper 1 through 4. Have students attach the paper to their personal clipboards.
2. Take the students on a walk to four specific areas. Some suggested areas are behind the cafeteria near the garbage bin, (yuk!); out on the playground just

after the grass has been mowed; near the cafeteria while lunch is cooking; in the parking lot. Instruct them to carefully observe the smells. Have them record (by drawing or writing) what they smell.
3. Return to the classroom and talk about the smells the students noticed, and the ones they recorded (see *Discussion*).
4. Ask the students who walk to school what pleasant smells they noticed along the way. Contrast this with the smells noticed by the students who came to school on the bus or in a car.
5. Point out that different smells remind us of different places.
6. Pass out the *My Home Smells Nice* student booklets and have the students draw or write about smells they can remember from home or assign this page for homework to discuss the following day.

Discussion
Part Two:

1. After returning from their walk, discuss with the students the types of smells they experienced: good, bad, earthy, wet, etc.
2. Ask the students to try to recall the smells they may have experienced on the way to school. Were the smells different for those who walked compared to those who rode in a bus or car? How were they different? How were they the same?
3. Discuss with the students how smells can remind us of things or events that happened in the past. You might want to bring in a scent of an evergreen tree, spray it and allow the students to smell it and ask them what it reminds them of. [Christmas] Other scents (potpourri) you might bring would be vanilla or cinnamon to remind students of things baking at home.
4. Discuss other smells the students may experience at home.
5. When they bring back their homework page showing their favorite smells from home, discuss the different smells and where the most pleasant smells were, and why.

Curriculum Correlation
Language Arts:
   see *Bibliography: Sense of Smell*

Home Links
   Send home the student book *My Home Smells Nice* for homework.

Our Smell Chart

	1	2	3	4

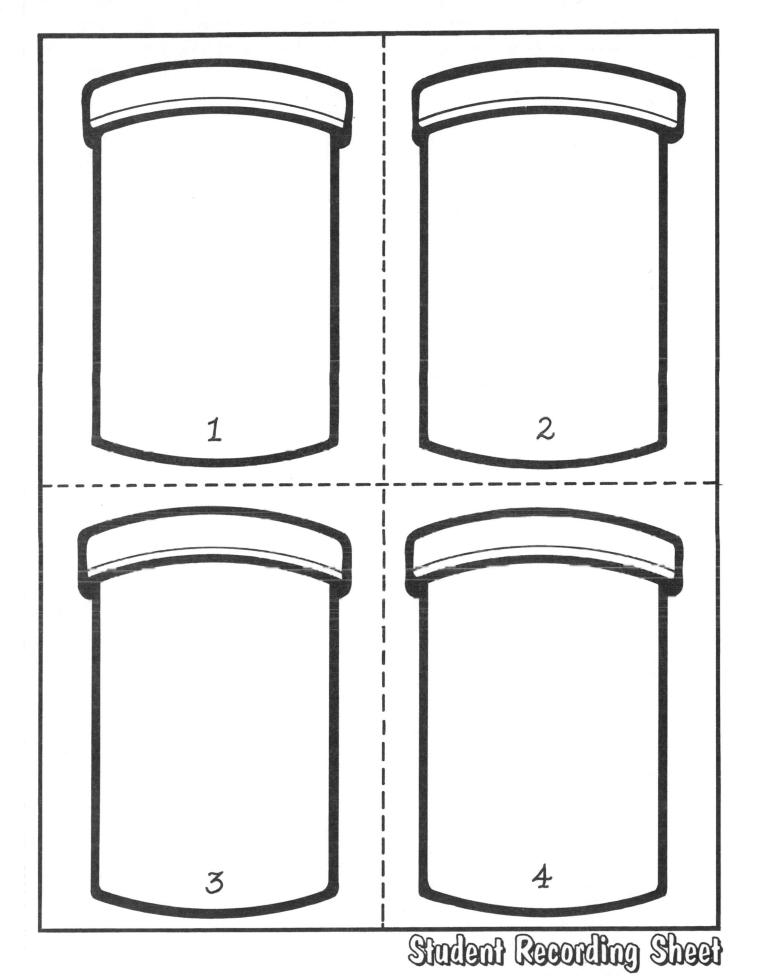

Student Recording Sheet

my

my

my

My
Home
Smells Nice

by

The Napping Nose

Topic
Sense of smell

Key Question
How long do you think you can smell the potpourri?

Learning Goal
Students will become aware of how the sense of smell becomes less sensitive to a scent with the passage of time.

Guiding Documents
Project 2061 Benchmarks
- *People use their senses to find out about their surroundings and themselves. Different senses give different information. Sometimes a person can get different information about the same thing by moving closer to it or further away from it*
- *Describing things as accurately as possible is important in science because it enables people to compare their observations with those of others.*

NCTM Standards 2000*
- *Count with understanding and recognize "how many" in sets of objects*
- *Sort and classify objects according to their attributes and organize data about the objects*
- *Represent data using concrete objects, pictures, and graphs*

Math
Graphing
Number sense and numeration
Measurement
    time

Science
Life science
    human senses

Integrated Processes
Observing
Comparing and contrasting
Predicting
Collecting and recording data
Interpreting data

Materials
Potpourri
Hot plate and pan or electric hot pot
Red construction paper (see *Management 1*)
Blue construction paper (see *Management 2*)
Glue or tape
Class graph (see *Management 5*)
Clock
Safety pins, one per student

Background Information
The nose smells through the use of the olfactory membrane which is located in the nasal passage just behind the bridge of the nose. This membrane is made up of sensory cells that send messages about scents via the olfactory nerve to the brain. The sensory cells in the olfactory membrane can become desensitized to the scents to which they are exposed over long periods of time. When you first walk into a room, you can smell many things: dinner cooking, perfume, flowers, smoke; but, after you have been in the room awhile, the olfactory nerves "get tired" and you no longer smell these odors.

Management
1. Prior to this activity, cut up 3/4" x 3/4" squares of red construction paper. You will need eight squares per student. The red construction paper is used to indicate that students can smell the potpourri.
2. Cut blue construction paper into 3/4" x 3/4" squares. You need one square per student. The blue construction paper is used to indicate that students cannot smell the potpourri.
3. Sticky notes may be used as an alternative to the cut-up squares of construction paper. The sticky notes would need to be cut to fit the chart.
4. Prepare the class chart by copying the provided sheets onto blue paper. Each sheet will accommodate 10 students. You will need to copy enough sheets for the number of students in your class. Any excess of squares should be cut off so the chart has one square along its horizontal axis for each student. Glue or tape the necessary sheets together. (If you want to enlarge the chart, you will also need to enlarge the red squares to fit.)

5. Prepare the chart as follows:
   a. the bottom of the chart should be numbered according to the number of students particiating in the activity
   b. draw in the hands on the clocks at 10 minute intervals
6. This activity takes one hour to complete. It is suggested that you plan either station work or group work that can be easily interrupted at 10-minute intervals (free exploration, manipulative discovery time, reading stories or books, show and tell, etc.)
7. Before school begins, put some potpourri in a hot pot and heat the pot to release the potpourri's scent.

Procedure
1. Have the whole class sit in a circle and discuss what is different in the room. [smell] Ask the *Key Question*: How long do you think you will be able to smell the potpourri?
2. Explain to the students what you have in the hot pot. Ask every student who can smell the scent to stand. For students who can smell the potpourri, pin a red square on their shirts and have them glue or tape a second red square on the bottom line of the class chart starting on the left side continuing to the right. If students cannot smell the potpourri, pin a blue square on them. These students will not need to place a square on the chart as the chart will show a blue space because of the lack of the red square.
3. Compare the amounts of blue spaces and red squares on the bottom line of the chart. (If all the students can detect the scent, the entire bottom line of the chart will be red squares with no blue chart paper showing.)
4. Tell the students to compare the red squares they are wearing to the red squares on the graph. Explain to them that the graph on the wall is a representation of our class. If they are all wearing red, then the graph at the *0 minutes* line should all be red. But if anyone can't smell the scent, there will not be a red square to represent that person. The graph will show blue space for that student.
5. At ten minute intervals, ask the students whether or not they can smell the potpourri. Those that can still smell it should put red squares on the appropriate line of the graph, always starting from the left and working to the right. Those that can't should exchange the red squares that are pinned on their shirts for blue squares. The students who do not smell the scent will add nothing to the graph because the blue automatically shows on the chart. Compare the amounts of red and blue showing on

the graph with the amounts of blue and red squares on the students' shirts.
6. At the end of an hour ask the students to sit in a large circle. Discuss how the number of people who could smell the potpourri changed and how the chart has comparatively changed.

Discussion
1. At the start of class, how many students put a red square on the *0 minute* line of the graph? How many students wore a red square at that time? What did that tell us? [everyone who could smell the potpourri wore a red square]
2. As the time passed in class, what happened to the color on our graphs and the squares on our shirts? [more became blue]
3. What does this tell us about the number of students who smelled the scent?
4. Have the students go outside the room for a short walk or recess. Upon coming back into the room, ask the students if they notice anything about the scent of the room. Count the number of students that can now smell the potpourri. Why do you think more of us can now smell the potpourri?
5. Why could we no longer smell the scent when it was still there? [We got used to it; our noses got "tired"] Explain that sometimes our olfactory sense gets desensitized, or "tired," and then we cannot smell something we smelled before.

Extensions
Visit the cafeteria near lunch time and note the different smells. Have students think about how long they can smell the cooking smells in the cafeteria when they go to lunch.

Curriculum Correlation
Literature:
    see *Bibliography: Sense of Smell*

Social Studies:
    How do smells keep us safe? [we can smell smoke that warns us of fire, we know by smell that there may be a gas leak, we can identify gasoline or rubbing alcohol by their smells and know that they are dangerous to us]

Home Links
Have students draw what they smell when they walk into their home after school. Ask Mom or Dad to help keep track (in minutes) of how long they can smell it.

* Reprinted with permission from *Principles and Standards for School Mathematics*, 2000 by the National Council of Teachers of Mathematics. All rights reserved.

The Napping Nose

60 minutes 🕐									
50 minutes 🕐									
40 minutes 🕐									
30 minutes 🕐									
20 minutes 🕐									
10 minutes 🕐									
0 minutes 🕐									

115

MAKING SENSE OF WHAT YOU SMELL

Topic
Sense of smell

Key Question
What sense can we use to tell things apart when they all look the same?

Learning Goal
Students will become aware of the importance of their sense of smell when confronted with objects that look the same.

Guiding Documents
Project 2061 Benchmarks
- *People use their senses to find out about their surroundings and themselves. Different senses give different information. Sometimes a person can get different information about the same thing by moving closer to it or further away from it*
- *Describing things as accurately as possible is important in science because it enables people to compare their observations with those of others.*

NCTM Standards 2000*
- *Count with understanding and recognize "how many" in sets of objects*
- *Sort and classify objects according to their attributes and organize data about the objects*
- *Represent data using concrete objects, pictures, and graphs*

Math
Charting

Science
Life science
   human senses

Integrated Processes
Observing
Comparing and contrasting
Predicting
Applying

Materials
For the class:
   extracts (examples: peppermint, lemon, orange)
   clay dough (see *Management 1*)
   red food coloring
   chart paper

For each student:
   white paper, 8.5 x 11-inch

Background Information
Our sense of sight often influences what we think things are. To convince young students that things are often not what they seem, it is necessary to challenge them with learning situations in which there is an imbedded surprise. Presenting young learners with items that are similar in appearance and texture, but have a different scent, is one way to do this. In this activity, students see and feel Clay Dough. It is then infused with various scents to help learners realize the importance of their sense of smell.

Management
Prior to the activity:
1. Make several batches of Clay Dough according to the recipe. Allow it time to cool and "cure." One recipe will make five balls of Clay Dough the size of tennis balls. You will need three balls for each group of six students.

Clay Dough
3 c. flour
1 1/2 c. salt
3 c. water
2 Tblsp. oil
3 tsp. cream of tartar

- Cook over low heat, stirring constantly until mixture is the consistency of mashed potatoes, and it begins to "lump."

- Remove from heat and knead, until a dough-like consistency is reached.
- Divide dough into balls the size of tennis balls.

2. Most dough will be used in its natural color; however, reserve a tennis-ball sized portion for each group. Color the reserved dough with red food coloring and scent it using lemon extract.

3. It is suggested that one group of six students work at this station while other students are engaged at other stations working on other activities.

4. Prepare a chart with the title *Making Sense of What You Smell*. Place several markers in the area for the recording of students' guesses.

Procedure

1. Introduce the uncolored, unscented Clay Dough to the group of students at the station. Have them look at and touch each of three balls to decide that they look and feel the same.

2. Make a "well" in each of the three balls of Clay Dough. Put 3-5 drops of one of the extracts into one ball. Knead the ball until the scent is spread throughout.

3. Follow the same procedure for the other two balls using the other two extracts.

4. Give each student a piece of paper. Tell them to fold it in half and then fold it in half again so they have 4 spaces. Have them number the spaces 1-4.

1	2
3	4

5. With one ball of scented Clay Dough, pinch off enough to give each student in the group a walnut-sized piece. Tell students to place this first Clay Dough ball in area numbered 1 on their paper. Do the same with the second ball of dough, having the students place their pieces in the area numbered 2, etc. Tell students not to mix the dough balls together.

6. Have the students smell the Clay Dough in area 1. Record their guesses as to what they think they are smelling on the chart paper. Continue with the Clay Dough in areas 2 and 3.

7. Show the students the Clay Dough you have colored and scented prior to classtime. Ask them to predict what the scent will be by simply looking at it. Record the predictions on the *Making Scents Of What You See* chart.

8. Give the students walnut-sized pieces of the red, scented Clay Dough to smell. Have them use area 4 on their sorting mats for this Clay Dough ball.

9. Ask students if they want to change their predictions and allow them to do so, if they wish.

10. After discussion, allow students to mold objects of their choice from the Clay Dough. Set them aside to dry.

Discussion

Using the unscented, non-colored Clay Dough balls:

1. Look at the Clay Dough. Do the three balls look the same?

2. Smell the Clay Dough. What does it smell like? Do all three balls of Clay Dough smell the same?

Using the scented, non-colored Clay Dough balls (one at a time):

3. Smell the Clay Dough. Do the three balls smell the same?

4. What scent do you think you are smelling? What does it remind you of? Continue until the students have examined all three Clay Dough balls.

5. Do all the clay dough balls look the same or different? How can you tell the difference between the three balls of Clay Dough? [by smelling them]

6. What sense did you use to name the scent of the Clay Dough balls? [sense of smell]

Using the colored, scented Clay Dough ball;

7. By using just your sense of sight, predict what scent this Clay Dough will be.

8. After smelling the Clay Dough ball, do you want to change your prediction or leave it the same?

9. Did the color help you make your prediction? Explain.

10. What happened when you used your sense of smell? Did your sense of smell help you determine the correct scent?

11. Did you guess the correct scent when you used just your sense of sight?…your sense of smell?… your senses of sight and smell?

12. If you had some Clay Dough that was orange and smelled like bananas, would you be able to name the scent? What does your sight do to your sense of smell?

13. Does your sense of smell or your sense of sight tell you what the scent of an object is?

14. If an object seems to be the wrong color, does it confuse our sense of smell?

Extensions

1. Use licorice (anise) extract in black Clay Dough at Halloween.

2. Color additional samples of Clay Dough a color that would be confusing with the scent added.

3. Add the sense of taste to the activity and use non-flavored gelatin. Add extract to the unflavored gelatin, and add food coloring that would again tend to confuse the student. For example: green-colored gelatin with orange-flavored extract.

Curriculum Correlation

Literature:

   see *Bibliography: Sense of Smell*

Making Scents From Scratch

(A Directed Art Activity)

Topic
"Scratch and sniff" art project

Materials
flavored gelatin and/or flavored crystal drink mix
white glue
student art page
plastic spoons
9-oz. plastic tumblers
optional: various flavors of extracts

Management
1. Set up a station or center for students to work independently or in small groups.
2. Put various flavors of the dry gelatin in 9-ounce plastic tumblers with a plastic spoon in each one.
3. Set out several bottles of white glue.
4. Either pass out student art pages (one per student) prior to the activity, or provide an ample supply of student art pages at the center for the students to use.

Procedure
1. Direct students to cover an area on their student art page with glue. They will then select the appropriate flavor of gelatin or crystal drink mix that depicts the fruit covered. For example: cover the strawberry picture with glue and then heavily sprinkle strawberry gelatin all over the surface of the glue. Allow to dry.
2. Once the glue has dried, you may want to add a drop of an extract to enhance the scent. Again, allow to dry.
3. Continue this process until all the pictures of fruit have been covered with the gelatin and glue.
4. Once the entire project is dried, direct the students to gently scratch the surface of one of the fruits and to then smell the scent.

118

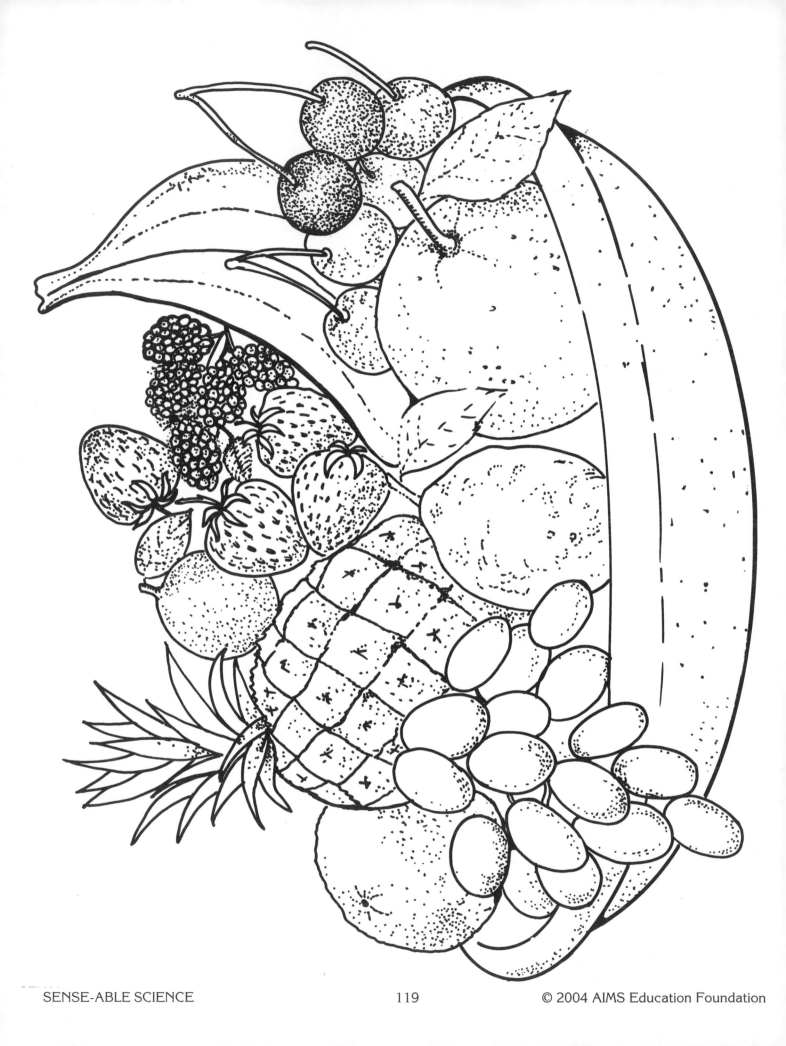

Hearing

It would seem that our hearing is reasonably sensitive. After all, we can adjust quickly to a great range of amplifications, from the sound of industrial noise to a friend's whisper a few seconds later. We can also hear a wide range of frequencies, from the low notes of a pipe organ to the high tones of a flute or piccolo. There are, however, many sounds that we humans cannot hear that other animals can. Bats have a much larger frequency range than humans. They use high frequency pitches to echolocate. Dogs can be summoned by blowing high frequency whistles which humans cannot hear. Animals such as donkeys and rabbits have large outer ears which they can move to pinpoint the source of a sound. We can do the same, although less precisely. If we hear a noise, we can turn our heads to pick up the strongest sound waves.

Hearing is important to everyday life. A large part of learning involves hearing. We learn to talk with all the proper inflections by listening to others, but people born with severly limited hearing have difficulty in learning to talk. Not only can they not hear the speech of others, but they cannot hear their own voice.

Human ears come in a remarkable variety of shapes and sizes. The outer flaps may not appear very complicated, but they play a very important role in how we interact with our world.

The outer ear flaps, called auricles, catch sound waves and funnel them into the auditory canal where a chain of events occur. The sound waves travel through the auditory canal where they strike the ear drum (tympanic membrane) and cause it to vibrate. The vibrations are passed on to three tiny bones in the middle ear called the hammer (malleus), the anvil (incus), and the stirrup (stapes). These bones transmit the vibrations to a membrane of the oval window which covers the opening of the inner ear.

The receptor cells for hearing are located within the inner ear. They are found in the cochlea which is a fluid-filled tube that contains hair-like receptors which respond to vibrations. The receptors send nerve signals to the brain where they are perceived as sound.

The hearing centers of the brain are located on both sides, just above the level of the ear. The brain begins building sound memories before birth. A baby in the womb can hear the sounds of its mother's heart beating and louder noises from outside. Gradually, sounds are linked with events; we connect the honking of a car's horn with danger, the creak of a door with someone entering the room, etc. Sounds are sorted out by the brain and compared with those in the memory. The brain then decides if the sound is important enough to act upon.

A Dryer Full Of Tennis Shoes

Brenda Dahl

When sounds are all around you,
It's hard to pick and choose.
You have to write a poem on sound—
What noises would you use?

The television's playing,
Someone's knocking at the door.
The dog is right beside you
Sleeping loudly on the floor.

A dryer full of tennis shoes
Is running in the hall;
The buzzer buzzes, cycle's done
You hear the gym shoes fall.

Your baby brother's crying,
Your pet parrot's in a rage,
He's squawking at the gardener
And pacing 'cross his cage.

Your mother yells, she'll sell him
If he doesn't quiet down.
You say your brother or the bird?
Imagining her frown!

A car horn says you're running late,
A clock's Westminster chime,
You're due at school in minutes
And your poem better rhyme!

What Can I Hear?

Tune: Billy Boy

Oh, what can I hear with my ears, with my ears?
Oh, what can I hear when I listen?
Children laughing, birds in trees,
Passing cars and buzzing bees;
These are sounds that I hear when I listen.

Oh, what can I hear with my ears, with my ears?
Oh, what can I hear when I listen?
Voices on the radio,
Someone walking very slow;
These are sounds that I hear when I listen.

Oh, what can I hear with my ears, with my ears?
Oh, what can I hear when I listen?
Airplanes flying overhead,
Something nice that someone said;
These are sounds that I hear when I listen.

Oh, what can I hear with my ears,
with my ears?
Oh, what can I hear when I listen?
Raindrops falling on my house
And the squeaking of a mouse;
These are sounds that I hear
when I listen.

Words by Suzy Gazlay

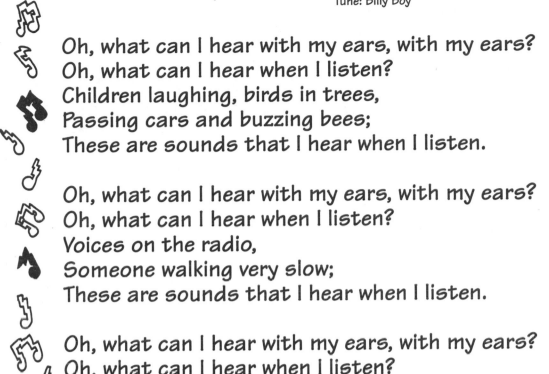

Secret Sounds

Topic
Sense of hearing

Key Question
What senses do we use to discover the contents of a sealed box?

Learning Goal
Students will use their sense of hearing to predict the contents of a set of sealed boxes.

Guiding Documents
Project 2061 Benchmarks
* *People use their senses to find out about their surroundings and themselves. Different senses give different information. Sometimes a person can get different information about the same thing by moving closer to it or further away from it*
* *Describing things as accurately as possible is important in science because it enables people to compare their observations with those of others.*

NCTM Standards 2000*
* *Count with understanding and recognize "how many" in sets of objects*
* *Sort and classify objects according to their attributes and organize data about the objects*
* *Represent data using concrete objects, pictures, and graphs*

Math
Graphing

Science
Life science
    human senses

Integrated Processes
Observing
Comparing and contrasting

Predicting
Collecting and recording data
Interpreting data

Materials
Part One
For the class:
    5 or more boxes with lids (examples: children's size shoe boxes, cheese boxes)
    5 pairs of small objects (see *Management 1*)
    class charts
    patterned wrapping paper or adhesive plastic, optional

For each student:
    glue
    yarn for student's book
    2 paper fasteners
    student activity sheet
    box template
    prediction markers
    student book

Part Two:
    scissors
    glue
    2 paper clips
    2 marbles
    2 small wooden blocks

Background Information
    Hearing is the sense which is second only to sight in the degree of development in humans. Our senses can be explored by isolating them and focusing on how each works. We can help students to fine-tune the use of their senses to aid in the discovery and learning of the world around them. Through this activity the students focus on hearing to discover information about objects that cannot be seen and are not touched.

Management

1. Collect 5 pairs of the small objects (toy cars, pennies, balls, jacks, unifix cubes).The duplicate object provides a point of reference as a visual clue for matching.
2. Beforehand, place one different object in each of the five boxes. Seal the boxes and number them, keeping record as to which object is in each box. To look more like gift boxes, you may wish to cover the boxes with wrapping paper or adhesive wrap.
3. This investigation can be used with the whole class or with small groups.
4. This investigation is divided into two parts. The first part uses teacher-prepared boxes while the second part uses student-prepared boxes.
5. Cut prediction markers (the pictures of the ball, the car, a jack, a penny, and the unifix cube) so each student, or group, will have the picture set of the five objects. (The do-it-yourself box which is also on that page will be used in *Part 2* of this investigation).

Procedure

Part One:

1. As an introduction to this investigation, read one of the suggested books listed in *Curriculum Correlation*. Discuss how difficult it is to wait to open gifts. How could you determine what your gifts are without opening them?
2. Show one of the boxes.
3. Guide students to decide which sense they could use to discover what is in the box.
4. As students respond, review which senses they would be using and discuss the use of the body part(s) associated with those senses.
5. Give each student a turn to handle the box and listen to the sounds the contents make as the box is moved back and forth.
6. Ask the students what, if anything, they can tell about the contents from just moving the box and listening. [sliding, rolling, forward movement, side movement]
7. Introduce the set of five objects to be used as a point of reference. These five objects **must** be identical to the five you previously wrapped in boxes.
8. Ask the students to observe the objects. Guide them to use the process of elimination in selecting their predictions of what could be in the box. By a show of hands, have students indicate what they think is in the first box.
9. Discuss the number of students predicting each object for the box shown. Direct students to place the picture of the predicted object in *Box 1* on their *Secret Sounds* activity page of gift-wrapped boxes.

10. Have a student open the box. Ask the students to check their predictions with the actual. If they were not correct in their predictions, instruct them to replace the markers with the correct markers. Direct all students to glue down the correct marker in *Box 1*.
11. Repeat the activity with other objects. Be sure to allow each student to handle the box, move it around and to listen to the sound made by the object in the box. Each time the options will get fewer. For *Box 5,* ask the students why they do not have to listen to the sounds the object makes.
12. Prepare a chart for the final actual results. You may want to use the prediction markers and boxes from the student pages for the legends of the chart. After the box is opened, record what was actually in the box. Use pictures or X's.

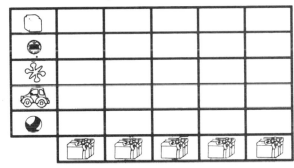

13. Ask students to draw a picture of one of the objects in the box on the activity page *In the box is a. . .* Use paper fasteners and yarn to tie the "box" together.

Discussion

Part One:

1. What clues were the most helpful in discovering the contents of the boxes? [Having objects as a frame of reference]
2. What sense did we use most to discover the contents?
3. How could we make the discovery easier? . . .harder?
4. Why do you think the _____ was easier to determine than the _____?
5. Why do you think the _____ was the hardest to determine?
6. Look at the shapes of the objects we used. What makes them easier (harder) to determine?
7. What other objects could we have used that would have been easy to predict by just listening to them in our boxes. [Bells]
8. What other objects could we have used that would have been hard to predict by listening to them?

Procedure

Part Two:

1. Have students fold and glue the do-it-yourself box. Glue all flaps except the one for the lid.
2. With students in small groups, ask one student to secretly place one of the three objects–paper clip, marble, or wooden block in the box. (Again, one set of the three objects will be displayed so the students have a reference set). This student will then gently move the box back and forth, allowing the other students to listen, but not to touch.
3. The other students will then predict what they think is in the box.
4. Once all students in the group have had a chance to express their predictions, direct the student who packed the box to open it and reveal the actual object.
5. You may want to use the student recording sheets (*Figure 2*) to either record their predictions or the actual objects.

Sounds like a ...

Sounds like a ...

Discussion

Part Two:

1. Was it harder to predict what was in these boxes than it was in the boxes with the cars, pennies, balls, jacks, and unifix cubes? Why or why not?
2. Was it easier when you got to handle the boxes and feel the objects move? Explain.
3. What sense did you use to determine what was in the boxes?

Extensions

1. Students make their own "secret boxes" to share with the class.
2. Discuss how different this activity would be if you had difficulty hearing. Apply this to everyday life for the hearing impaired. This could lead to learning about similarities and differences of people.

3. Ask one student to hide behind a closed door. Instruct another student to listen to the hidden student's voice and determine who is behind the door.

Curriculum Correlation

Literature:

1. Read books about all kinds of containers and packages. Some suggestions:
    Gino and Linda Alberti, *The Red Parcel*
    Eric Carle, *The Secret Birthday Message*
    David A. Carter, *Bugs in a Box*
    David A. Carter, *More Bugs in a Box*
    Jean M. Craig, *The Dragon in the Clock Box*
    Harriet Ziefert, *The Big Birthday Box*
    Charlotte Zolotow, *Mr. Rabbit and the Lovely Present*
2. see *Bibliography: Sense of Hearing*

Home Links

1. Have the students play a guessing game with their parents. With one family member behind a door, ask another person to listen to the voice to try to determine who is hiding. The same game can be played using objects that make noise.
2. Create "secret boxes" as a family project to share at home or take to school.

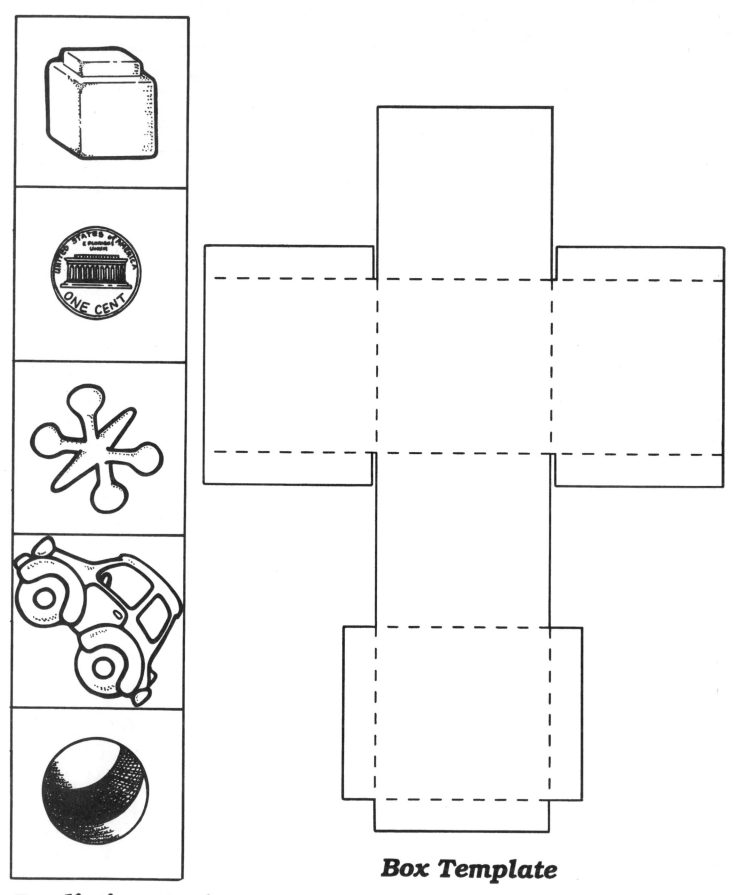

Prediction Marker

Box Template

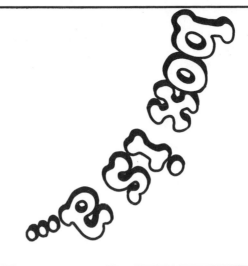

Sounds like a ...

Sounds like a ...

WALK, STOP & LISTEN

Topic
Sense of hearing

Key Question
What can our ears tell us about our school?

Learning Goal
Students will become aware of information they gather through their sense of hearing.

Guiding Documents
Project 2061 Benchmarks
- *People use their senses to find out about their surroundings and themselves. Different senses give different information. Sometimes a person can get different information about the same thing by moving closer to it or further away from it*
- *Describing things as accurately as possible is important in science because it enables people to compare their observations with those of others.*

NCTM Standards 2000*
- *Count with understanding and recognize "how many" in sets of objects*
- *Sort and classify objects according to their attributes and organize data about the objects*
- *Represent data using concrete objects, pictures, and graphs*

Math
Charting
Equalities and inequalities

Science
Life science
    human senses

Integrated Processes
Observing

Comparing and contrasting
Classifying
Collecting and recording data
Interpreting data

Materials
For the class:
    felt pens
    class chart, enlarged

For each student:
    personal blindfold (see *Appendix: Science Tools*)
    paper
    crayons

For each cross-age tutor:
    paper
    pencil
    personal clipboard (see *Appendix: Science Tools*)

Background Information
    The brain begins building sound memories before birth. A baby in the womb can hear the sounds of its mother's heart beating and louder noises from outside. Gradually, sounds are linked with events; we connect the honking of a car's horn with danger, the creak of a door with someone entering the room, etc. Sounds are sorted out by the brain and compared with those in the memory. The brain then decides if the sound is important enough to act upon.

Management
1. Cross-age tutors are necessary for this activity. The tutors will need to be trained in order to serve as sighted guides for the younger students.
2. Upper-grade students will serve as guides for blindfolded younger students. The younger students will

be lead by the older students to four different areas around the school (examples: office, cafeteria, all-purpose room, library). Younger students will walk one step behind their sighted guides, holding onto the guides' arms just above the elbows.

3. Prepare recording sheets by folding paper into fourths and numbering each section. Instruct the sighted guides that each section is a designated area that will be visited. Assign a number, 1-4, for each area. The guides will record the younger students' responses from each area in the appropriately numbered section of the paper.
4. Enlarge the class chart showing one section for each of the areas which have been selected for visiting.
5. If personal blindfolds have not been previously made, make them prior to doing this activity.
6. The sighted guides will use the personal clipboards (directions found in *Appendix: Science Tools)* for writing on during the blindfolded tour.

Procedure

1. Practice listening with students in the classroom. Discuss the many sounds they hear.
2. Rehearse the sighted-guide technique with the students without using the blindfolds.
3. Distribute recording sheets, pencils, and clipboards to the sighted guides.
4. The sighted guides will blindfold their younger student partners and escort them to a specified location where they will stop and sit still for two minutes to listen. The guides are not to tell the various locations. Younger students then tell their guides what they hear and where they think they are. The guide writes down the responses in the appropriately numbered section of the recording sheet. All four specified areas are done in the same manner.
5. Upon returning to the classroom, blindfolds are removed and the guides review the younger students' responses which were recorded in each area.
6. Each younger student draws a picture of whatever made the sound he or she liked best.
7. Post the pictures on the class chart in the appropriate area (1, 2, 3, or 4) where the sound was heard.

Discussion

1. What did you hear?
2. What can you tell about stop number one?…two?… three?…four?
3. How were the sounds at stop one different from the sounds at stop two?
4. How were the sounds the same?
5. Did you need your eyes to tell where you were? Explain.
6. By looking at our chart, can we name the places we went?
7. Make a list of all the sounds we heard at stop number one…two…three…four.
8. At which area did our class find their favorite sounds?…the least favorite sounds? Why do you think this was so?

Extensions

1. Take the students outside, blindfold them, and have them sit on the playground for a few minutes before recess begins. Discuss the sounds. Have them continue to sit while the bell rings and other classes come outside for recess. Discuss the differences heard before, during, and after recess.
2. Have the students go into the cafeteria during lunch. Seat them at a table, put on blindfolds, and listen to the sounds of the cafeteria as the different classes come and go. After lunch, discuss all the sounds the students can recall hearing.
3. Tape record an entire listening walk. After returning to the classroom, listen to the tape and discuss what made the sounds heard on the tape.

Curriculum Correlation

Language Arts:
    Write about the sounds. Use sentences such as: My favorite sound was _____. I did not like the ____ sound.

Art:
    Draw a picture of whatever produces their favorite sound.

Social Studies:
    Discuss other sounds heard in the home and around the community.

Home Links

    Give students two 3" x 5" cards or pieces of paper to take home. Have them draw their favorite home sounds and bring the pictures back to class to make a class chart.

* Reprinted with permission from *Principles and Standards for School Mathematics,* 2000 by the National Council of Teachers of Mathematics. All rights reserved.

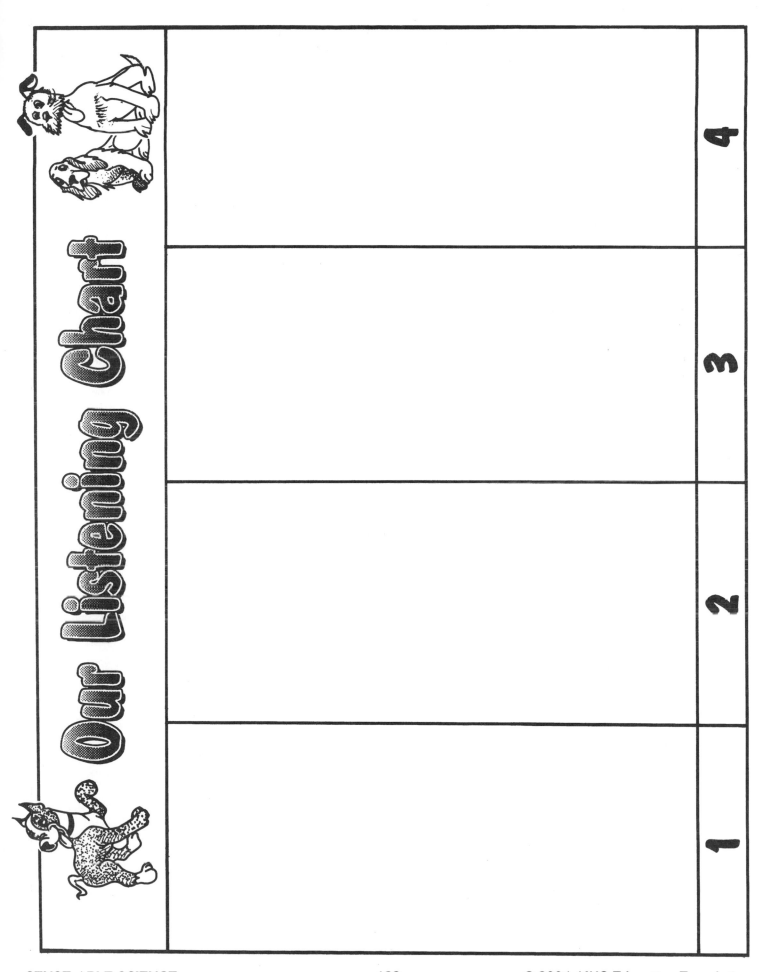

Our Listening Chart

1	2	3	4

Designer  Ears

Topic
Sense of hearing

Key Question
How does the size and shape of ears make a difference in how well we hear?

Learning Goals
Students will:
1. create models of various shaped ears and
2. determine which is most effective.

Guiding Document
Project 2061 Benchmarks
- *People use their senses to find out about their surroundings and themselves. Different senses give different information. Sometimes a person can get different information about the same thing by moving closer to it or further away from it*
- *Describing things as accurately as possible is important in science because it enables people to compare their observations with those of others.*
- *Some animals and plants are alike in the way they look and in the things they do, and others are very different from one another.*
- *Plants and animals have features that help them live in different environments.*

Science
Life science
　　human senses

Integrated Processes
Observing
Comparing and contrasting
Inferring
Applying

Materials
For each group of four students:
　　kitch timer that ticks
　　various-sized cups made from different materials
　　construction paper
　　tape
　　scissors
　　animals pictures

Background Information
Sound travels through the air in waves which spread out from the source of the sound. When a sound is produced, some of the sound waves will reach your ears, but most of them are spread out into the surrounding area. When you cup your ear with your hand, you are actually channeling more of the sound waves into your outer ear.

Many animals have ears that are better designed to pick up sounds than are human ears. These animals tend to have more cup-shaped and/or proportionally larger ears than we humans have. Many also have the advantage of being able to turn their ears which helps them locate the direction of sounds. Humans must turn their heads to do this.

Management
1. Prior to this activity, make one or two models of cup-ears for demonstration.
2. This activity works well with four students per group.
3. In this activity, students will use construction paper and cups of various materials to design cup "ears" to channel sound waves into their ears.
4. Throughout this activity, continually remind students not to put anything inside their ears. The "designer ears" will all be held to the outside of the outer ear.
5. Use the pictures provided with this activity or search out pictures of animals from magazines.

Procedure
1. Give each group cups of various sizes and materials (plastic, paper, Styrofoam) and construction paper.
2. Ask the *Key Question*. Allow students time to brainstorm how they could design "ears" that would enable them to hear better.
3. Show the students the pictures of animals. What do you notice about their ears? [some have ears open to the sides of their heads, some to the fronts; some ears can turn; some are big; some are covered, some are open]
4. After students have brainstormed several ideas, show the "ears" you constructed. Tell the students that they can use the cups, construction paper, scissors, and glue to design different ears. They will test the effectiveness of these designs by listening to a kitchen timer.

Discussion
1. When you tested the different ears that you designed, what shapes did you find that helped you to hear better?
2. Does the size of the ear make a difference? Explain.
3. Does the type of material the ear is made of make a difference? What material worked best for you? Why do you think it worked best?
4. Name an animal that has very good hearing. How do you know this? What shape are its ears?
5. Which of the ears that you designed remind you of animal ears? Which animals?

Extension
Study animals and their hearing. Research information about animals that have a keen sense of hearing compared to those which do not. What are the differences in the sizes and shapes of their ears.

DIRECTION DETECTION

Topic
Sense of hearing

Key Questions
1. Do we really need both ears to hear?
2. Do we need both ears to locate where the sound is coming from?

Learning Goal
Students will discover that they can hear sounds using only one ear, but that it is easier to locate the source of sounds around them when they use both ears.

Guiding Documents
Project 2061 Benchmarks
- *People use their senses to find out about their surroundings and themselves. Different senses give different information. Sometimes a person can get different information about the same thing by moving closer to it or further away from it*
- *Describing things as accurately as possible is important in science because it enables people to compare their observations with those of others.*

NCTM Standard 2000*
- *Count with understanding and recognize "how many" in sets of objects*

Math
Counting
Tallying

Science
Life science
    human senses

Integrated Processes
Observing
Comparing and contrasting
Collecting and recording data
Interpreting data
Inferring
Applying

Materials
For each group of four students:
    2 pennies
    transparent tape
    2 crayons of different colors

For each student:
    student blindfolds (see *Appendix: Science Tools*)
    rabbit tally piece

Background Information
When you cover one of your ears, you can still hear. Then why do we have two ears? This activity will demonstrate to the students that they can hear with only one ear, but the two ears working together help them to determine where the sounds they are listening to are coming from.

When you are listening with both ears, sounds reach the ear closest to it a split second before reaching the other ear. In addition, the sound in the closer ear is slightly louder since the head interferes with the sound reaching the other ear. When one ear is covered, you cannot usually use these slight differences in sound speed and volume to locate the sound source.

Humans have binaural hearing; that is, we use two ears to hear. People with hearing in only one of their ears many have difficulty locating sounds. They might need to turn their heads in several directions before finding the source of the sound.

Management
1. It is not recommended that students share blindfolds because of the possible exposure to eye diseases. If personal blindfolds are not already made, use the pattern in the *Appendix* and make prior to doing this activity.
2. This activity begins with a demonstration of procedures. The class is then divided into groups of four. One student will be the *Direction Detector,* another student will be the evaluator to determine whether the guess is *Right On* or *Way Off,* a third student will be the recorder, and a fourth student will be the castanet player.

3. The clapping of penny castanets will be used as sound sources. Penny castanets are made by taking a small strip of tape (large enough to fit around the end of your finger) and making a circle with the sticky side on the outside. A penny is then stuck onto the tape. Each group will need two of these penny devices. One will be placed over the thumb and one over the forefinger of the same hand.

4. Copy the tally records, one per student. Students will record by tallying the *Direction Detectors* results. *Right On* will be tallied on the rabbit's upright ear. *Way Off* will be tallied on the floppy ear.
5. Set standards for determining whether guesses are *Right On* or *Way Off.*

Procedure

1. To demonstrate the procedure for the class, have students sit in a large circle. Select a student, the *Direction Detector*, to sit in a chair that is placed in the middle of the circle.
2. Blindfold the *Direction Detector* making certain not to cover his/her ears. Caution students to be very, very quiet because you will be using penny castanets to make a sound. The *Direction Detector* will then try to point in the direction of the location of the sound. Tell the *Direction Detector* not to turn his or her head.
3. Place the castanets on your forefinger and thumb. Quietly walk to a location in the room and click the pennies twice. The *Direction Detector* is to point in the direction he/she believes you are standing. Continue by moving to different locations.
4. To demonstrate the tallying component of this activity, mark each *Right On* guess by the *Direction Detector* on the rabbit's upright ear and each *Way Off* guess on the floppy ear. Review tallying by making four marks and showing the fifth mark as a diagonal across the existing four. Use one color for two-ear results. (The other color will be used for one-ear results.)

5. After several attempts, direct the *Direction Detector* to press one finger or the palm of his/her hand against one ear, closing off the ear canal and preventing sound waves from entering.
6. Repeat the above procedures, moving to different locations, clicking twice and recording the results with the second color.
7. Divide the class into groups of four. Allow students to rotate jobs until each student has an opportunity to be the *Detection Detector*.
8. Have each student experience the activity using both ears and then covering one. Record the results.
9. Have students tape their tally records on the wall. Have students count the number of *Right On* results …*Way Off* results. Record these results on the chalkboard.

Discussion

1. What do our tally records tell us about this experience?
2. Were there more *Right On* responses?
3. Was it harder to determine the location of the source of sound with only one ear? Why do you think that way?
4. What do you think people who can only hear out of one of their ears do to help them hear better? [they turn their heads toward the sounds to hear better]
5. Why would it be important to know the source of a sound? [warnings of danger: sirens, barking dogs]

Extension

Click the pennies directly in front of the blindfolded person. Do the same directly behind, and on top of his/her head. Is the person confused? When the sound comes from a spot midway between the ears, it reaches both ears at the same time, making it hard to figure out where the sound is coming from.

* Reprinted with permission from *Principles and Standards for School Mathematics*, 2000 by the National Council of Teachers of Mathematics. All rights reserved.

STUDENT TALLY PIECE

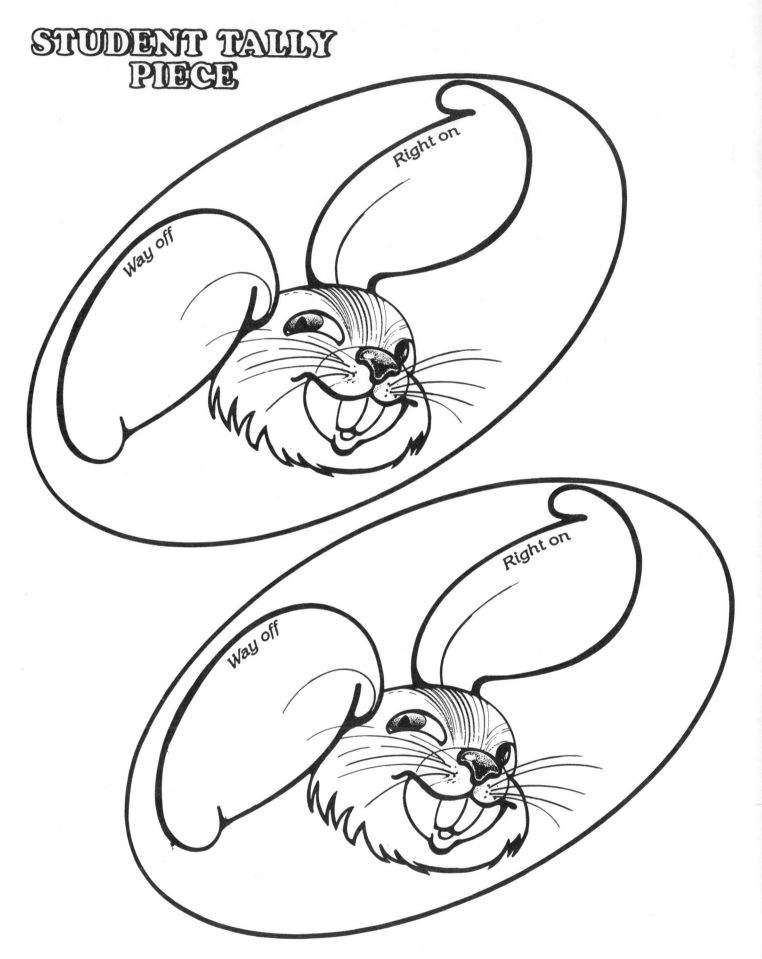

Way off

Right on

Way off

Right on

PAPER PICNIC

Topic
Human senses

Key Question
What senses do we use when we go on a picnic?

Learning Goal
Students will create a book of picnic items and identify which of the five senses can be experienced with each food item.

Guiding Documents
Project 2061 Benchmark
- *People use their senses to find out about their surroundings and themselves. Different senses give different information. Sometimes a person can get different information about the same thing by moving closer to it or further away from it*
- *Describing things as accurately as possible is important in science because it enables people to compare their observations with those of others.*

NCTM Standards 2000*
- *Count with understanding and recognize "how many" in sets of objects*
- *Sort and classify objects according to their attributes and organize data about the objects*
- *Represent data using concrete objects, pictures, and graphs*

Math
Charting
Graphing
Tallying

Science
Life science
  human senses

Integrated Processes
Observing
Comparing and contrasting
Classifying
Predicting
Collecting and recording data
Interpreting data
Applying

Materials
For the class:
  stapler
  enlarged graph
  chart paper

For each student:
  precut pages for *A Sense-able Picnic* book
  tally page
  10 pieces of white paper, 2 x 2 inches
  markers, crayons, or colored pencils
  pencils and erasers
  scissors
  glue

Background Information
By this time, students should have an understanding of what the five senses are and how each is unique and important. This activity will be used as a culminating experience to reinforce that understanding and to further strengthen the concept that most often our senses are used simultaneously to give us more complete information about our world.

Management
1. Prior to the lesson make a chart entitled *Our Sense-able Picnic* and enlarge the *Our Sense-able Picnic* graph. Copy one *Picnic Tally* page per student.
2. Prepare a five-column bar graph. Label the columns with the large five senses labels across the bottom.
3. Prepare the materials for the *My Sense-able Picnic* book. The amount of preparation is dependent upon the needs of your class. You may choose

138

to use the blackline masters accompanying this lesson, or you may choose to have your students create their own pages.

4. This activity can be done over a period of days, depending on the makeup of your class, your adult helper/child ratio, and your own teaching style. Just be sure that the initial brainstorming and the final graphing activities are done with the whole group. The book construction can occur during center time, at learning-stations, or as a whole group.

Procedure

Whole Class Instruction:

1. Introduce the chart and tell the students that you are going to go on a pretend picnic. This picnic will be a five senses picnic. Invite them to brainstorm foods they might take on the picnic which they can see, hear, smell, taste, and touch. Record the responses on the chart while students describe the senses they would use to experience the food items on the picnic.

2. Introduce the *Five Senses* student book. Tell the students that there are certain requirements for deciding what to take on this picnic:
   • they are to be sure to include one item for each of the five senses
   • all items must be edible
   • all items must fit into a picnic basket.

3. Allow the students to offer suggestions as to how they should proceed. [one sense per day; two senses today, three tomorrow, etc.]

4. Have the students cut and staple the prepared pages together.

5. Distribute the 2" x 2" pieces of paper. The students need to draw two pictures of each of the foods they have decided to pack in their picnic baskets–one item per piece of paper. One picture will be used for the book, the second will be used on a class graph.

6. Have the students glue one set of pictures onto the top tabs of the book. The tabs will show over the top of the basket, displaying pictures of all the items packed for the picnic.

7. Direct students to complete the sentences on the pages of the book by writing in or drawing the food they decided to include for that sense.

8. In a large group discussion setting, challenge students to see how many of the items initially suggested appeared in their books.

9. After sharing the items that appear in the students' books, begin the process of graphing using a five-column bar graph. Each time someone suggests a food, decide which sense(s) are used to experience this food. Instruct the students to use the second set of pictures they drew to graph the contents of their picnic basket. (Some students may put a peanut butter sandwich in the sight column,

others put it in the smell column, yet others might put it in the touch column.) Guide the students to generalize that each of the five senses (with a few exceptions) can apply to any food that could be taken on a picnic.

10. Once the graphing has been completed, direct students to tally the results. For those students developmentally ready, instruct them to record the numeral representing the tallied amount on the right side of the page. Discuss the results.

Discussion

1. Have students compare the brainstorm charts made during the original discussion and the graph, then ask: Did anyone put the items from our brainstorm list in their books? How could you tell? Name three items that you used from the list in your book?

2. Did anyone use different foods for their picnic book? What were they?

3. What kind of food items should we put together to make a very, very noisy lunch? (Try to include something that is a fruit, something that is a vegetable, something that is a bread or a cracker, something to drink, and some meat or cheese.)

4. What food item do you think would have the best smell? Do you think everyone agrees with that? Why or why not?

5. Which sense do you think is the most important when going on a picnic? Do you think everyone agrees? Why or why not?

6. According to our graph, was a particular food always assigned to the same sense by everyone in the class? Explain.

7. Using our tally sheet, did everyone record their answers? How do we know this? [if everyone recorded one food per each of the five senses, there should be the same number of tallies in each section]

Extensions

1. Have each of the students bring a snack item to school. Chart or graph what has been brought, then go on a "snack picnic."

2. Have the students repeat the activity, but this time in small collaborative groups.

Curriculum Correlation

Literature:
   see *Bibliography:* all senses

---

*   Reprinted with permission from *Principles and Standards for School Mathematics*, 2000 by the National Council of Teachers of Mathematics. All rights reserved.

Name	Picnic Tally	Total
See		
Hear		
Smell		
Touch		
Taste		

© 2004 AIMS Education Foundation

Our Sense - able Picnic

		Taste
		Touch
		Smell
		Hear
		See

See

Hear

Taste

Smell

Touch

My Sense - able Picnic

In my picnic
basket,
I see

1

2

In my picnic basket, I hear

In my picnic
basket,
I smell

In my picnic
basket, I taste

5

3

4

In my picnic basket, I feel

Science tools

Patterns for student blindfolds

- Because of the possibility of the spread of eye diseases through sharing blindfolds, we highly recommend that each student be provided with a personal blindfold.
- Duplicate the blindfolds onto card stock.
- Direct students to use crayons, markers, stickers, etc. to decorate their blindfolds.
- Laminate each blindfold for durability.
- Use hole punch to make a hole on either side of the blindfold.
- Reinforce the holes so they don't tear out with use.
- Attach elastic or two strong strings.

© 2004 AIMS Education Foundation

Field Trip Clipboards

These clipboards can be taken on walking or riding field trips. Students or helpers can use them as study supports to record experiences, reactions, or comments made during the explorations.

- Cut a 9" x 12" piece of heavy cardboard. (Recycle those boxes!)
- Cover the front and back of the cardboard with adhesive-backed paper. Seal the edges.
- To add more support, use masking tape to frame the edges all around.
- Attach two large paper clips to the top of the clipboard for holding an 8 1/2" x 11" piece of paper.
- Cut a 24" length of string, cord, or yarn. Tie one end around a sharpened pencil. Secure the string to the pencil with masking tape. Knot the other end of the string and attach it to the back of the clipboard with masking tape.

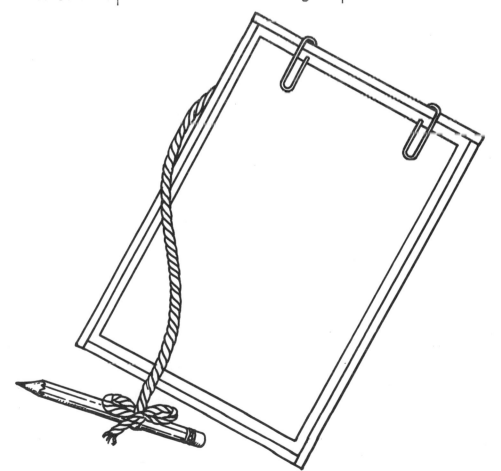

Bibliography

Teacher Resource
Ardley, Neil. *The Science Book of Color.* Gulliver Books. Harcourt Brace Jovanovich. NY.1991.
Parker, Steve. *Touch, Taste and Smell.* Franklin Watts, Inc. NY. 1991.
Parker, Steve. *The Ear and Hearing.* Franklin Watts, Inc. NY. 1991.
Parker, Steve. *The Eye and Seeing.* Franklin Watts, Inc. NY. 1989.
Parker, Steve. *Touching a Nerve: How You Touch, Sense and Feel.* Franklin Watts, Inc. NY. 1992.
Silverstein, Alvin, Virginia and Robert. *Smell, The Subtle Sense.* Morrow Junior Books. NY. 1992.
Taylor, Barbara. *Seeing Is Not Believing!* Random House. NY. 1990.
Van Der Meer, Ron and Atie. *Amazing Animal Senses.* Little Brown and Company. Boston.1990.

The Sense of Sight
Brown, Ruth. *If At First You Do Not See.* Henry Holt and Company. NY. 1982.
Carle, Eric. *Brown Bear, Brown Bear, What Do You See?* Henry Holt. NY. 1983.
Ehlert, Lois. *Planting A Rainbow.* Harcourt Brace Jovanovich. NY. 1988.
Fowler, Allan. *Tasting Things.* Children's Press. NY. 1991.
Freeman, Don. *A Rainbow Of My Own.* Viking Press. NY. 1966.
Hoban, Tana. *Dots, Spots, Speckles, and Patterns.* Greenwillow Books. NY. 1987.
Kim, Joy. *Rainbows and Frogs.* Troll Associates. New Jersey.1981.
Lankford, Mary. *Is It Dark? Is It Light?* Knopf. NY. 1991.
Martin, Bill and John Archambault. *Knots Of A Counting Rope.* Holt.NY. 1987.
Micklethwait, Lucy. *I Spy Two Eyes, Numbers In Art.* Greenwillow Books. NY. 1992.
Micklethwait, Lucy. *I Spy, An Alphabet In Art.* Greenwillow Books. NY. 1991.
Rosen,Michael. *We're Going On a Bear Hunt.* Macmillan. NY.1992.
Smith, Lane. *Glasses, Who Needs 'em?* Viking Press. NY. 1991.
Stinson, Cathy. *Red Is Best.* Annick Pres. NY. 1982.
Tsujimoto, Aileen. *Now I Wear Glasses.* Heian International, Inc. Union City, CA. 1990.
Walsh, Ellen Stoll. *Mouse Paint.* Harcourt Brace Jovanovich. NY. 1989.
Williams, Sue. *I Went Walking.* Harcourt Brace Jovanovich. NY. 1989.

The Sense of Touch
Aliki. *My Hand.* Harper Trophy. 1990.
Blackstein, Karen. *The Blind Men and the Elephant.* Schoolastic. NY.1992.
Dorros, Arthur. *Feel The Wind.* Thomas Crowell. NY. 1989.
Holzenthaler, Jean. *My Hand Can.* Dutton Childrens Books. NY. 1978.
Moncure, Jane Belk. *The Touch Book.* Children's Press. Chicago. 1982.
Silverman, Erica. *Warm In Winter.* Macmillan. NY. 1989.
Wood, Nicholas. *Touch . . . What Do You Feel?* Troll Associates. NY. 1991.

The Sense of Taste
Allington, Richard L. and Kathleen Krull. *Tasting.* Raintree Steck- Vaughan. 1985.
Carle, Eric. *The Very Hungry Caterpillar.* Scholastic Book Services. NY. 1974.
Dooley, Norah. *Everybody Cooks Rice.* Carolrhoda Books, Inc. Minneapolis. 1991.
Fowler, Allan. *Tasting Things.* Chicago Press. Chicago.1991.
Marshall, Jones. *Goldilocks and The Three Bears.* Dial Books. NY. 1988.
Moncure, Jane Belk. *A Tasting Party.* Children's Press. Chicago. 1982.
Seuss, Dr. *Green Eggs and Ham.* Random House. NY. 1960.

Seuss, Dr. *Scrambled Eggs Super!* Random House. NY. 1953.
Sharmat, Mitchell. *Gregory The Terrible Eater*. Scholastic. NY. 1980.
Smith, Kathie B. and Victoria Crenson. *Tasting*. Troll Books. 1987.
Tolhurst, Marilyn. *Somebody and the Three Blairs*. Orchard Books. NY.1990.
Turkle, Brinton. *Deep In The Forest*. Dutton Children's Books. NY. 1976.

The Sense of Smell
Allington, Richard L. and Kathleen Krull. *Smelling*. Raintree Steck- Vaughan. 1985.
Carter, Noelle and David. *Merry Christmas Little Mouse*. Holt. NY. 1993.
Fowler, Allan. *Smelling Things*. Children's Press. Chicago. 1991.
Howard, Katherine. *Little Bunny Follows His Nose*. A Golden Book. NY. 1971.
Krauss, Ruth. *The Happy Day*. Harper Childrens Books. NY. 1949.
Smith, Kathie B. and Victoria Crenson. *Smelling*. Troll Associates. NY. 1988.

The Sense of Hearing
Baylor, Byrd. *The Other Way To Listen*. Macmillan. NY. 1978.
Brown, Margaret Wise. *The Noisy Book*. Harper Trophy.1993.
Brown, Margaret Wise. *The Quiet Noisy Book*. Harper Trophy.1993.
Browne, Anthony. *Bear Hunt*. Doubleday. NY.1990.
Carle, Eric. *The Very Quiet Cricket*. Philomel Books. NY. 1990.
Fowler, Allan. *Tasting Things*. Childrens Press. NY. 1991.
Fox, Mem. *Night Noises*. Harcourt Brace Jovanovich. NY. 1989.
Grindley, Sally. *Shh!* Little Brown and Company. Boston. 1991.
Hines, Anna Grossnickle. *Thumble, Thumble, Boom*. Greenwillow Books. NY, 1992.
Levi, Dorothy Hoffman. *A Very Special Sister*. Kendall Green Publications. Washington,D.C. 1992.
Martin, Bill, Jr. and Eric Carle. *Polar Bear, Polar Bear What Do You Hear?* Henry Holt and
    Company. NY. 1991.
Martin, Bill, Jr. and John Archambault. *Listen To the Rain*. Henry Holt and Company. NY. 1988.
Perkins, Al. *The Ear Book*. Random House. NY. 1968.
Peterson, Jeanne Whitehouse. *I Have A Sister My Sister Is Deaf*. Harper   Trophy. NY. 1977.
Spier, Peter. *Crash! Bang! Boom!* Doubleday. Japan. 1972.
Spier, Peter. *Gobble, Growl, Grunt!* Doubleday. Japan. 1980.
Showers, Paul. *Ears Are For Hearing*. Harper Trophy. NY. 1990.
Witty, Bruce. *Noise In The Night*. School Zone Publishing Company. Grand Haven, MI. 1991.

Multi-Sensory
Aliki. *My Five Senses*. Harper and Row. 1989.
Heide, Forence Parry. *The Day of Ahmed's Secret*. Lothrop. NY. 1990.
Hutchins, Pat. *Changes, Changes*. Aladdin Books. NY.
Lionni, Leo. *Frederick*. Knopf. NY. 1967.
Martin, Bill and John Archambault. *Here Are My Hands*. Holt. NY. 1987.
McMillan, Bruce. *Super, Super, Super Words*. Lothrop Lee and ShepardBooks. NY. 1989.
McPhail, David. *Farm Morning*. Harcourt Brace Jovanovich. NY. 1991.
Selsam, Millicent and Joyce Hunt. *Keep Looking!* Macmillan. NY. 1989.
Showers, Paul. *The Listening Walk*. Harper Trophy. 1993.
Tresselt, Alvin. *Wake Up, Farm!* Lothrop. NY. 1991.

The AIMS Program

AIMS is the acronym for "Activities Integrating Mathematics and Science." Such integration enriches learning and makes it meaningful and holistic. AIMS began as a project of Fresno Pacific University to integrate the study of mathematics and science in grades K-9, but has since expanded to include language arts, social studies, and other disciplines.

AIMS is a continuing program of the non-profit AIMS Education Foundation. It had its inception in a National Science Foundation funded program whose purpose was to explore the effectiveness of integrating mathematics and science. The project directors in cooperation with 80 elementary classroom teachers devoted two years to a thorough field-testing of the results and implications of integration.

The approach met with such positive results that the decision was made to launch a program to create instructional materials incorporating this concept. Despite the fact that thoughtful educators have long recommended an integrative approach, very little appropriate material was available in 1981 when the project began. A series of writing projects have ensued and today the AIMS Education Foundation is committed to continue the creation of new integrated activities on a permanent basis.

The AIMS program is funded through the sale of this developing series of books and proceeds from the Foundation's endowment. All net income from program and products flows into a trust fund administered by the AIMS Education Foundation. Use of these funds is restricted to support of research, development, and publication of new materials. Writers donate all their rights to the Foundation to support its on-going program. No royalties are paid to the writers.

The rationale for integration lies in the fact that science, mathematics, language arts, social studies, etc., are integrally interwoven in the real world from which it follows that they should be similarly treated in the classroom where we are preparing students to live in that world. Teachers who use the AIMS program give enthusiastic endorsement to the effectiveness of this approach.

Science encompasses the art of questioning, investigating, hypothesizing, discovering, and communicating. Mathematics is a language that provides clarity, objectivity, and understanding. The language arts provide us powerful tools of communication. Many of the major contemporary societal issues stem from advancements in science and must be studied in the context of the social sciences. Therefore, it is timely that all of us take seriously a more holistic mode of educating our students. This goal motivates all who are associated with the AIMS Program. We invite you to join us in this effort.

Meaningful integration of knowledge is a major recommendation coming from the nation's professional science and mathematics associations. The American Association for the Advancement of Science in *Science for All Americans* strongly recommends the integration of mathematics, science, and technology. The National Council of Teachers of Mathematics places strong emphasis on applications of mathematics such as are found in science investigations. AIMS is fully aligned with these recommendations.

Extensive field testing of AIMS investigations confirms these beneficial results.

1. Mathematics becomes more meaningful, hence more useful, when it is applied to situations that interest students.

2. The extent to which science is studied and understood is increased, with a significant economy of time, when mathematics and science are integrated.

3. There is improved quality of learning and retention, supporting the thesis that learning which is meaningful and relevant is more effective.

4. Motivation and involvement are increased dramatically as students investigate real-world situations and participate actively in the process.

We invite you to become part of this classroom teacher movement by using an integrated approach to learning and sharing any suggestions you may have. The AIMS Program welcomes you!

AIMS Education Foundation Programs

A Day with AIMS®

Intensive one-day workshops are offered to introduce educators to the philosophy and rationale of AIMS. Participants will discuss the methodology of AIMS and the strategies by which AIMS principles may be incorporated into curriculum. Each participant will take part in a variety of hands-on AIMS investigations to gain an understanding of such aspects as the scientific/mathematical content, classroom management, and connections with other curricular areas. *A Day with AIMS®* workshops may be offered anywhere in the United States. Necessary supplies and take-home materials are usually included in the enrollment fee.

A Week with AIMS®

Throughout the nation, AIMS offers many one-week workshops each year, usually in the summer. Each workshop lasts five days and includes at least 30 hours of AIMS hands-on instruction. Participants are grouped according to the grade level(s) in which they are interested. Instructors are members of the AIMS Instructional Leadership Network. Supplies for the activities and a generous supply of take-home materials are included in the enrollment fee. Sites are selected on the basis of applications submitted by educational organizations. If chosen to host a workshop, the host agency agrees to provide specified facilities and cooperate in the promotion of the workshop. The AIMS Education Foundation supplies workshop materials as well as the travel, housing, and meals for instructors.

AIMS One-Week Perspectives Workshops

Each summer, Fresno Pacific University offers AIMS one-week workshops on its campus in Fresno, California. AIMS Program Directors and highly qualified members of the AIMS National Leadership Network serve as instructors.

The AIMS Instructional Leadership Program

This is an AIMS staff-development program seeking to prepare facilitators for leadership roles in science/math education in their home districts or regions. Upon successful completion of the program, trained facilitators may become members of the AIMS Instructional Leadership Network, qualified to conduct AIMS workshops, teach AIMS in-service courses for college credit, and serve as AIMS consultants. Intensive training is provided in mathematics, science, process and thinking skills, workshop management, and other relevant topics.

College Credit and Grants

Those who participate in workshops may often qualify for college credit. If the workshop takes place on the campus of Fresno Pacific University, that institution may grant appropriate credit. If the workshop takes place off-campus, arrangements can sometimes be made for credit to be granted by another institution. In addition, the applicant's home school district is often willing to grant in-service or professional-development credit. Many educators who participate in AIMS workshops are recipients of various types of educational grants, either local or national. Nationally known foundations and funding agencies have long recognized the value of AIMS mathematics and science workshops to educators. The AIMS Education Foundation encourages educators interested in attending or hosting workshops to explore the possibilities suggested above. Although the Foundation strongly supports such interest, it reminds applicants that they have the primary responsibility for fulfilling *current* requirements.

For current information regarding the programs described above, please complete the following:

Information Request

Please send current information on the items checked:

____ *Basic Information Packet* on AIMS materials   ____ *A Week with AIMS®* workshops
____ *AIMS Instructional Leadership Program*   ____ Hosting information for *A Day with AIMS®* workshops
____ *AIMS One-Week Perspectives* workshops   ____ Hosting information for *A Week with AIMS®* workshops

Name _____   Phone_____

Address _____
        Street   City   State   Zip

We invite you to subscribe to AIMS Magazine

Each issue of the magazine contains a variety of material useful to educators at all grade levels. Feature articles of lasting value deal with topics such as mathematical or science concepts, curriculum, assessment, the teaching of process skills, and historical background. Several of the latest AIMS math/science investigations are always included, along with their reproducible activity sheets. As needs direct and space allows, various issues contain news of current developments, such as workshop schedules, activities of the AIMS Instructional Leadership Network, and announcements of upcoming publications. *AIMS the Magazine* is published monthly, August through May. Subscriptions are on an annual basis only. A subscription entered at any time will begin with the next issue, but will also include the previous issues of that volume. Readers have preferred this arrangement because articles and activities within an annual volume are often interrelated.

Please note that a subscription automatically includes duplication rights for one school site for all issues included in the subscription. Many schools build cost-effective library resources with their subscriptions.

YES! I am interested in subscribing to AIMS Magazine

Name _____   Home Phone _____

Address _____   City, State, Zip _____

Please send the following volumes (subject to availability):

_____Volume IX (1994-95) $10.00   _____Volume XIV (1999-00) $35.00

_____Volume X (1995-96) $10.00   _____Volume XV (2000-01) $35.00

_____Volume XI (1996-97) $10.00   _____Volume XVI (2001-02) $35.00

_____Volume XII (1997-98) $10.00   _____Volume XVII (2002-03) $35.00

_____Volume XIII (1998-99) $35.00   _____Volume XVIII (2003-04) $35.00

_____**Limited offer: Volumes XVIII & XIX (2003-2005) $60.00**

(Note: Prices may change without notice)

Check your method of payment:

☐ Check enclosed in the amount of $_____

☐ Purchase order attached (Please include the P.O.#, the authorizing signature, and position of the authorizing person.)

☐ Credit Card ☐ Visa ☐ MasterCard   Amount $ _____

Card # _____   Expiration Date _____

Signature _____   Today's Date _____

Make checks payable to **AIMS Education Foundation.**
Mail to AIMS Magazine, P.O. Box 8120, Fresno, CA 93747-8120.
Phone (559) 255-4094 or (888) 733-2467 FAX (559) 255-6396
AIMS Homepage: http://www.aimsedu.org/

AIMS Program Publications

Actions with Fractions 4-9
Awesome Addition and Super Subtraction 2-3
Bats Incredible! 2-4
Brick Layers 4-9
Brick Layers II 4-9
Chemistry Matters 4-7
Counting on Coins K-2
Cycles of Knowing and Growing 1-3
Crazy about Cotton Book 3-7
Critters K-6
Down to Earth 5-9
Electrical Connections 4-9
Exploring Environments Book K-6
Fabulous Fractions 3-6
Fall into Math and Science K-1
Field Detectives 3-6
Finding Your Bearings 4-9
Floaters and Sinkers 5-9
From Head to Toe 5-9
Fun with Foods 5-9
Glide into Winter with Math & Science K-1
Gravity Rules! Activity Book 5-12
Hardhatting in a Geo-World 3-5
It's About Time K-2
It Must Be A Bird Pre-K-2
Jaw Breakers and Heart Thumpers 3-5
Just for the Fun of It! 4-9
Looking at Geometry 6-9
Looking at Lines 6-9
Machine Shop 5-9
Magnificent Microworld Adventures 5-9
Marvelous Multiplication and Dazzling Division 4-5
Math + Science, A Solution 5-9
Mostly Magnets 2-8
Movie Math Mania 6-9
Multiplication the Algebra Way 4-8
Off The Wall Science 3-9
Our Wonderful World 5-9
Out of This World 4-8
Overhead and Underfoot 3-5
Paper Square Geometry:
    The Mathematics of Origami
Puzzle Play: 4-8
Pieces and Patterns 5-9

Popping With Power 3-5
Primarily Bears K-6
Primarily Earth K-3
Primarily Physics K-3
Primarily Plants K-3
Proportional Reasoning 6-9
Ray's Reflections 4-8
Sense-Able Science K-1
Soap Films and Bubbles 4-9
Spatial Visualization 4-9
Spills and Ripples 5-12
Spring into Math and Science K-1
The Amazing Circle 4-9
The Budding Botanist 3-6
The Sky's the Limit 5-9
Through the Eyes of the Explorers 5-9
Under Construction K-2
Water Precious Water 2-6
Weather Sense:
    Temperature, Air Pressure, and Wind 4-5
Weather Sense: Moisture 4-5
Winter Wonders K-2

Spanish/English Editions*

Brinca de alegria hacia la Primavera con las
    Matemáticas y Ciencias K-1
Cáete de gusto hacia el Otoño con las
    Matemáticas y Ciencias K-1
Conexiones Eléctricas 4-9
El Botanista Principiante 3-6
Los Cinco Sentidos K-1
Ositos Nada Más K-6
Patine al Invierno con Matemáticas y Ciencias K-1
Piezas y Diseños 5-9
Primariamente Física K-3
Primariamente Plantas K-3
Principalmente Imanes 2-8

*   All Spanish/English Editions include student pages in Spanish and
    teacher and student pages in English.

Spanish Edition

Constructores II: Ingeniería Creativa Con Construcciones LEGO® (4-9)
    The entire book is written in Spanish. English pages not included.

Other Science and Math Publications

Historical Connections in Mathematics, Vol. I 5-9
Historical Connections in Mathematics, Vol. II 5-9
Historical Connections in Mathematics, Vol. III 5-9
Mathematicians are People, Too
Mathematicians are People, Too, Vol. II
Teaching Science with Everyday Things
What's Next, Volume 1, 4-12
What's Next, Volume 2, 4-12

For further information write to:
AIMS Education Foundation • P.O. Box 8120 • Fresno, California 93747-8120
www.aimsedu.org/ • Fax 559•255•6396

AIMS Duplication Rights Program

AIMS has received many requests from school districts for the purchase of unlimited duplication rights to AIMS materials. In response, the AIMS Education Foundation has formulated the program outlined below. There is a built-in flexibility which, we trust, will provide for those who use AIMS materials extensively to purchase such rights for either individual activities or entire books.

It is the goal of the AIMS Education Foundation to make its materials and programs available at reasonable cost. All income from the sale of publications and duplication rights is used to support AIMS programs; hence, strict adherence to regulations governing duplication is essential. Duplication of AIMS materials beyond limits set by copyright laws and those specified below is strictly forbidden.

Limited Duplication Rights

Any purchaser of an AIMS book may make up to *200 copies* of any activity in that book for use at *one school site*. Beyond that, rights must be purchased according to the appropriate category.

Unlimited Duplication Rights for Single Activities

An individual or school may purchase the right to make an unlimited number of copies of a single activity. The royalty is $5.00 per activity per school site.

Examples: 3 activities x 1 site x $5.00 = $15.00
9 activities x 3 sites x $5.00 = $135.00

Unlimited Duplication Rights for Entire Books

A school or district may purchase the right to make an unlimited number of copies of a single, *specified* book. The royalty is $20.00 per book per school site. This is in addition to the cost of the book.

Examples: 5 books x 1 site x $20.00 = $100.00
12 books x 10 sites x $20.00 = $2400.00

Magazine/Newsletter Duplication Rights

Those who purchase *AIMS®* (magazine)/*Newsletter* are hereby granted permission to make up to 200 copies of any portion of it, provided these copies will be used for educational purposes.

Workshop Instructors' Duplication Rights

Workshop instructors may distribute to registered workshop participants a maximum of 100 copies of any article and/or 100 copies of no more than eight activities, provided these six conditions are met:

1. Since all AIMS activities are based upon the *AIMS Model of Mathematics* and the *AIMS Model of Learning*, leaders must include in their presentations an explanation of these two models.
2. Workshop instructors must relate the AIMS activities presented to these basic explanations of the AIMS philosophy of education.
3. The copyright notice must appear on all materials distributed.
4. Instructors must provide information enabling participants to order books and magazines from the Foundation.
5. Instructors must inform participants of their limited duplication rights as outlined below.
6. Only student pages may be duplicated.

Written permission must be obtained for duplication beyond the limits listed above. Additional royalty payments may be required.

Workshop Participants' Rights

Those enrolled in workshops in which AIMS student activity sheets are distributed may duplicate a maximum of 35 copies or enough to use the lessons one time with one class, whichever is less. Beyond that, rights must be purchased according to the appropriate category.

Application for Duplication Rights

The purchasing agency or individual must clearly specify the following:
1. Name, address, and telephone number
2. Titles of the books for Unlimited Duplication Rights contracts
3. Titles of activities for Unlimited Duplication Rights contracts
4. Names and addresses of school sites for which duplication rights are being purchased.

NOTE: Books to be duplicated must be purchased separately and are not included in the contract for Unlimited Duplication Rights.

The requested duplication rights are automatically authorized when proper payment is received, although a *Certificate of Duplication Rights* will be issued when the application is processed.

Address all correspondence to: **Contract Division**
AIMS Education Foundation
P.O. Box 8120
Fresno, CA 93747-8120

www.aimsedu.org/
Fax 559•255•6396

AIMS Data Organizers

In response to popular demand, AIMS is introducing a set of six data organizers. The open-ended design gives teachers flexibility and eases preparation for a variety of data-gathering activities. Each 23" x 35" organizer is intended for classroom display. Corresponding blackline masters are also included.

- The *2-Circle Venn* is a standard way to show two sets in which some members of each set share common attributes.
- The *Column Graph/Chart* can be used as a pictograph, a chart, or, if lines are added, a table to record data. We offer 2-Column and 3-Column Graph/Charts.
- The *Graph Grid* can become a bar graph, a line graph, a class data table, or a record of geometric patterns. It is designed to accommodate small sticky notes.
- The *Circle/Percent* graph, marked in 1% increments, makes the production of pie graphs much easier and also doubles as a single-circle Venn diagram.
- The *Binary Tree* is useful for classifying objects, persons, leaves, etc. to show their uniqueness.

The upcoming *Sense-able Science* publication is including some titles and labels specifically for these organizers. Future AIMS books may incorporate their use from time to time.

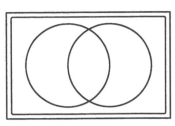
2-Circle Venn

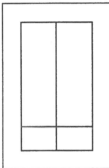
2-Column Graph/Chart

3-Column Graph/Chart

Suggestions For Use

To make a reusable data organizer

- Laminate it first.
- Use water-soluble pens.
- Write or stick on title, labels, numbers, and/or art.
- When you are through displaying the data, remove all art, labels, etc.
- Wipe off pen markings with damp paper towel.
- Use the data organizer for a different activity.

To make a permanent data organizer

- Add the title, labels, numbers, and graphics before laminating.
- Use water-soluble pens to record class data.
- When finished, wipe off the data with a damp paper towel.
- Use it for the same activity the next time you introduce it.

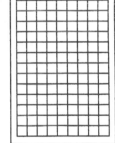
Graph Grid

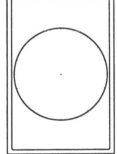
Circle/Percent Graph

Ordering Information

Item No.	Organizer Description	Price
1501	Data Organizer Sampler (1 of each)	$12.95
1502	2-Circle Venn Diagram (set of 6)	$12.95
1503	2-Column Graph/Chart (set of 6)	$12.95
1504	3-Column Graph/Chart (set of 6)	$12.95
1505	Graph Grid (set of 6)	$12.95
1506	Circle/Percent Graph (set of 6)	$12.95
1507	Binary Tree (set of 6)	$12.95

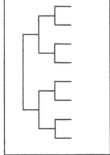
Binary Tree

Please add a 10% shipping and handling fee. California residents must add applicable local sales tax.